CW01627986

How To Get A

JOB IN FORMULA 1

The ULTIMATE guide to jobs and careers in F1

By Stephen Sawyer

Orders: Please visit **www.jobsinf1.com** to place orders for this book.

British Library Cataloguing in Publication Data
A catalogue record for this title is available from the British Library.

ISBN 978-1910202005

First published 2014

Typeset by the Book Publishing Academy

Printed in Great Britain by Bell and Bain for Quetop Consulting Limited, Matrix House 12-16 Lionel Road, Canvey Island, SS8 9DE.

Quetop Consulting Limited policy is to use papers that are natural, renewable and recyclable products and made from wood grown in sustainable forests.

The logging and manufacturing process are expected to conform to the environmental regulations of the country of origin.

Disclaimer

Every effort has been made to ensure the information contained within this product is accurate at the time of publication. Quetop Consulting Limited or the author is not responsible for anyone failing to achieve a career in formula one in any capacity as a result of the information supplied within this guide. Quetop Consulting Limited and the author cannot accept any responsibility for any errors or omissions within this guide, however caused. No responsibility for loss or damage occasioned to any company, organisation or person acting, or refraining from action, as a result of the material in this publication can be accepted by Quetop Consulting Limited or the author.

Quetop Consulting Limited and the author are not responsible for any financial loss, injury or death sustained as a result of the pursuit of a career in formula one, or as a result of any of the information contained within this guide. It is the responsibility of the user to ensure that he/she has validated themselves any and all information independently.

The information contained within this guide does not represent the views of any third party service or organisation.

Contents

1. INTRODUCTION

Welcome to the world of F1 and "How To Get A Job In Formula 1".

This guide has been designed to give you inside tips to help prepare you for a career in Formula 1, and to give you step by step instruction to follow for your racing or engineering career preparation, with details of the preferred qualifications and educational facilities recognised by the F1 teams. I explain in detail how to build your network connections to progress your career, how to write a CV and how to prepare for the interview.

My name is Stephen Sawyer and I am the author of this book. I have spent in excess of 24 years working in the motorsport and automotive industry and have held positions from apprentice to company director. I have developed some of the worlds most advanced vehicle safety systems used in supercars and volume production cars, written several specifications and conducted many interviews.

I have led many engineering teams to develop complete vehicles from concept, through development and into production, and have an in depth knowledge of complete vehicle design, vehicle and systems testing, quality processes and systems. I have built and prepared both single seat and saloon cars that won their championships; and provided guidance to some of the most recognised drivers in motor sport.

I provide services as a senior consultant in advanced technologies, and have managed government funded research projects specialising in all electric and hybrid vehicle technologies, including vehicle ECU's, electric motor design, energy recovery, battery energy storage and vehicle control systems since 2008. All of these systems are now part of a modern F1 car.

A career is not something that happens overnight; and you have to make a clear plan of how your career should progress and this book has been written in useful sections to prepare you for each stage. Read each section carefully and take notes as you progress through the process of planning your career.

While the selection process for a job in formula one is highly competitive, there are a number of things you can do to improve your chances of success, and they are all contained in this book.

Whether you want to be a driver, an engineer, or work in the supporting business, don't ever give up on your dream. The effort required is exactly the same for an F1 team as it is to do that job in any other company in the motorsport and automotive industry. The way to prepare for a job is to embark on a programme of in-depth preparation, and this guide shows you how to do that.

Work hard, stay focused, and live the dream.

With Kind Regards

Stephen Sawyer

2. PREFACE

By author Stephen Sawyer

When I started my career I had little to no guidance on how to build a career in motorsport, let alone know how to get a job in Formula 1.

Being the only member of my immediate family with any interest in the sport, getting support from my parents was hard because they had no knowledge of the motorsport industry, and they had their own ideas of what type of career I should study. It took a real determination to steer my career and put it on the right track.

I always believed that success is a result of preparation, and this is also what will help you be successful. I had to find my way around the hard way, researched what to study, where to study and figure out how to enrol for courses. I worked really hard to get experience whilst studying, and even harder to make my own contacts. I paid a lot of money to learn how to write a really good CV and cover letter, learnt how to research jobs and companies, and figured out how to get an interview, and then how to impress at an interview. Eventually after 15 years of effort I got to work at McLaren where I held the position of Function Group Leader responsible for all technical development, test validation, commercial, quality activities and resources within my department. This position enabled me to be involved in many interesting development activities across the McLaren companies.

I really enjoy my career, and there are many people who would like to be part of F1, but like me had no idea how to get a job in F1; so I have written this book all about the jobs that exist in the F1 companies to help you plan your career and to save you a considerable amount of time and effort. It explains a simple step-by-step guide to becoming an F1 driver, getting a job as an engineer, or working in many of the other roles and doing something you really do dream about.

The book contains information that will enable you to establish your formula one pedigree and set you apart from other candidates. You will find a lot of information regarding the types of jobs and roles within a formula one company and the qualifications required. It explains how to educate yourself, where to educate yourself and how to tick the boxes that F1 teams are looking to fulfil, and increase your opportunities of being selected for an interview and getting a job in F1.

Everybody starts somewhere and everyone has a slightly different story to tell, in my case I worked in the peripheral formulas building cars and designing solutions, and working in the automotive industry designing supercars. I would never be afraid to try new ideas for fear of failure because failure is simply a building block to refining success and how you apply that knowledge. Preparation and planning is the key to mitigating failure, enhanced by knowledge of the subject matter, so please ensure you prepare yourself for your career.

This book is published in both paper and eBook versions. It contains hyperlinks to further information to save you time and effort. By using this book in conjunction with the **www.jobsinf1.com** website it will expedite your learning and career planning. If you are reading the paperback version there is information that you need access to and it changes on a regular basis, obviously we cannot update published paper books, but we can offer that service on the internet and you can get access to our contacts and frequent updates of new jobs for all of the teams via the members area of the website.

You will find a lot of useful technical information about F1 car design as well as other information that will help you to build your knowledge of formula one.

My advice is to read the book, carry out the actions described and use the website to save you time and effort.

3. ACKNOWLEDGEMENT

I would like to honour the generations of drivers and engineers that preceded me and formed my passion for Formula 1. I hold dear an admiration for those competing today, and I look forward to being witness to the ingenuity and talent of the future generation of drivers and engineers, I would like to commend all of the people that give their time and talent to supporting Formula 1 and making the sport the incredible global success that it has become.

I would like to say thank you to all of the amazing and incredible people that have contributed to my career and to the lecturers that forged my education and have taken the time to ensure that I thoroughly understood the course materials. To all of the of the managers that helped me to turn the academic knowledge in to practical applications and gave me the opportunity to demonstrate my potential and ability, and allowed me to lead teams of engineers; to those colleagues that I share my time with, who not only have been a pleasure to work with but also contributed to my success and have also become life long friends.

What I find truly inspiring is how a team can bond and work for each other, and the high level of professionalism and respect that is shared between colleagues, how everyone is prepared to listen and discuss every challenge, this is why Formula 1 motor sport and the automotive industry is at the leading edge of technical development and contributes so much to world engineering.

Finally, I would like to thank my family for their support and guidance, their understanding, and allowing me to pursue my career, for taking care of each other while I travelled with my work. I would like to dedicate this book to my wife who has given me an inner strength, she is my rock, and to my children who give me the will and determination to succeed.

4. RESEARCHING A CAREER IN F1

CHOOSING YOUR CAREER

If you are looking for a job in F1 you should invest a bit of time in researching the types of job you would like to perform and the type of job you are capable of performing. We have all dreamt at one point or another of being a Formula 1 driver but may not have the skill and finances to compete and do the job.

We need to explain that **www.Jobsinf1.com** is a website dedicated to helping you find your dream job in F1 and works in conjunction with book. The website allows your learning to be interactive with other users and if there is information that you would like to know you may request it. A great way to get involved is to use the social media connections and to invite your friends with a common interest to take part.

Depending on the type of role you choose to pursue you need to understand what kind of qualification and education you need. In this book we have focused on becoming an F1 driver and an engineer, but there are numerous peripheral jobs within the formula one industry and we have listed these jobs in this book.

Whilst most of the teams are based in the UK occasionally you do from time to time get a team that sets themselves up in mainland Europe, and as F1 moves into new territories we may see new teams entering the circus. So if you are considering a career in F1 you have to be prepared to live where the work is done unless you are looking to work at a circuit or in the local media.

Each of the F1 teams has its own website, however the quality and the content of information on their websites does vary considerably. Although you will be able to find the contact details of each of the team's headquarters on their website, some of the teams also publish open vacancies that they have within the team, but what you need to consider, is that this is the first place people looking for a job in formula one will visit, this is not the only way to get a job in formula one .

Through the team's own website, they will receive several inquiries in relation to any one vacancy, and this could run into several hundred applications. What you have to appreciate is the F1 teams and their HR departments cannot necessarily invest a significant amount of time in trawling through each and every one of those inquiries to the fullness of its content because, in all honesty, not everybody that applies for a job is potentially capable. Just because they are a fan and watch every race does not make them a candidate for a job as an F1 engineer.

You may be requested to complete an online registration along with the other applicants, if your CV is not formatted correctly or if you have not used the correct terminology or keywords in your CV or cover letter, you will be whittled out of contention before the person conducting the interview even gets a CV to review. An initial review of a CV is just 7-15 seconds long.

Fortunately there are other routes to a job in formula one. Many of the teams use a preferred agency or a contracting house in order to help them whittle down the applications to the right candidate for the job or to find someone with experience.

The danger that you have is unless your CV is correctly formatted and includes the correct kind of key words that will draw the attention of a HR person or recruitment agent, you will just get lost in the volume. And by applying to an F1 team, you really only have the one chance to get it right, if you're not picked, then you may be added to a database, but you may never go further than that.

The other route is to use one of the preferred agencies or a contracting house. Now, these companies will obviously look at several of the positions that are available, they would have already monitored the F1 sites in order to determine the vacancies available, they will have a list of preferred candidates, and what you would find is that by establishing a relationship with one of these agencies or contracting houses and by talking to them, you'll be able to pick up feedback that will help you to optimise your CV in order to get it noticed by the recruiter.

WHAT IS AN AGENCY?

A recruitment agency will have a contract with a company to find resource, filter through the CV's and propose candidates. The agency will be paid a one off fee for any successful vacancy filled. The successful candidate will be hired as an employee or contractor of the F1 company. Each F1 Team has its own preferred recruitment agents and it is worthwhile investing some time researching which companies support the teams.

WHAT IS A CONTRACTING HOUSE?

A contracting house collects CV's like a recruiter but they provide the required services to the F1 teams and will put a contractor to work at the F1 company charging an hourly fee or daily rate for the amount of on going service provided. This is usually with the intention of fulfilling a short fall in resource or skill set. Contracts could last anywhere from 1 month, and usually build in blocks of 3 months up to 1 year.

DIRECT CONTRACTORS

Several F1 companies don't like to carry the overhead of employees and so therefore they employ the services of contractors in order to support the ramp up of design activities. These people accept a short-term period of work that could last as long as a year.

Typically a contractor would be a CAD designer, this is somebody that uses computer aided design in order to create geometry and drawings, or to run simulations based on a set of criteria determined by the lead engineer. They would create the 3D CAD model and a 2D drawing that would then be modelled as a 3D prototype and trialled on a model in the wind tunnel or sent to a supplier for manufacture.

Typically CAD skills in CATIA, Pro Engineer, Solidworks, are required and these are the main tools used by F1 teams and suppliers.

Other key skills required are those people with experience of new technologies or manufacturing processes, specialised materials experience or someone versed in ensuring quality of parts. Mathematics, science and software combined is a powerful tool to the modern F1 team as analysts play an ever increasing role in race simulation.

Some of these contractors work independently and they will have a direct relationship with the F1 company. These would be individuals with a good track record and reputation in the industry. In other cases these people are hired through preferred recruitment agencies for a finding fee but are contracted directly by the team.

Needless to say, it is obviously far more profitable for a contractor if they have a direct relationship with the company, because then they are not supporting the finding fees and overhead cost of the agency. It also puts the contractor in a position to negotiate their own terms of contract rather than those dictated by an agent.

Each F1 team has its own preferred contract agencies based on the quality of person they have been supplying to the team, and probably for a number of years. It is worthwhile registering your CV with these agencies but it is essential that you CV is prepared correctly and optimised to work with the agencies IT tools. In order to learn how to prepare your CV please see the chapter creating a great CV.

It is unlikely that a contractor will hold any senior position in an F1 company. If you wish to remain with a team and develop a career you will need to become an employee. But placement by an agent or contracting house may be your first route into F1 and provide an opportunity to demonstrate your skills and experience.

CONSULTANTS

From time to time a consultant may be hired, this is an experienced or knowledgeable individual that would advise a specific course of action to overcome a particularly difficult challenge. This may be someone with a PhD Doctorate in an engineering discipline. e.g. a chemical engineer for a specific material composition. A consultant can demand a high daily rate.

USING YOUR NETWORK

Find out who you know that works in Formula 1, motorsport or the automotive industry, find out what they do, how and where they studied. Ask friends, family, work colleagues who they know. Buy magazines, go to trade shows, go racing and network the pit lane, use the Internet, pick up the phone, but most importantly make new contacts, it is easy to stay in the same social circle but network onwards and upwards. Collect business cards and write on the back where and when you met, this will help you to remember them in the future.

USE THE JOBS IN F1 NETWORK

We have built a Formula 1 social network to help you expand yours. This can be accessed by using the **www.jobsinf1.com** website. Click the "Follow Us" Social Media Icon buttons on the home page and subscribe to the website. We have provided a Facebook, Google +, Twitter, LinkedIn and Tumblr pages to make sure you have a platform to gain exposure, and the members area will accelerate your contact list and keep you informed of the latest jobs and news articles. In the members area you will find a significant number of contacts.

5. EDUCATION EXPLAINED

The question that follows "how do you get a job in F1" is what qualifications do you need? The challenge to explain this was always to find the qualifications for students in their home country, for secondary schools and university, without being too generic. F1 fans live all over the world, studying in many languages and disciplines.

In this chapter we give you an overview of the UK education system and explain how students from all over the world can gain a comparable education recognised by education authorities and industry across the world, and acknowledged by F1 teams.

JUNIOR SCHOOL EDUCATION

Primary education starts aged 7 years and covers the subjects of literacy, numeracy, mathematics, science, geography, history, physical education and music, but excludes a second language.

SATS (Standard Assessment Tests) grade tests are given at the end of 2nd, 6th and 9th year of a pupil's education to determine a student's progress against children of their own age.

The levels of progress in primary education are as follows:

Level W Working towards level 1, very weak,

Level 1 Average for a typical 5 years old,

Level 2 Average for a typical 7 years old,

Level 3 Average for a typical 9 years old,

Level 4 Average for a typical 11 years old.

11 +

The 11 Plus is an exam taken by pupils in their last year of primary education aged 11 years to determine which type of secondary school they could attend. This is not offered to all pupils and candidates are selected by the teachers and heads of year.

SECONDARY SCHOOL EDUCATION IN THE UK

At this point we need to explain how the remaining levels of UK education qualifications compare, while this may be familiar to many in the UK, foreign schools, colleges and universities have comparable international qualifications, and the Open University offers comparable courses for foreign students with an "I" preceding the UK qualification i.e. a GCSE becomes an IGCSE. Non UK students can also look at the European Qualification Framework.

The choice of secondary school's are:

1. Grammar School

Grammar school is intended for the top 25 percent of intellectually capable pupils and teaches an academic curriculum. Typical courses studied include: Mathematics, English, Science, IT, Art, Music, Drama, French and German (one of them very intensively to GCSE standard), Latin, History, Geography, Religious Education (RE), Physical Education (PE), Personal Social Health Education (PSHE), Technology, Literature, and separate Biology, Physics and Chemistry, RE.

2. Comprehensive School or Secondary Modern

A Comprehensive or Secondary School is intended to teach the populous Mathematics, ICT, English, RE, Citizenship, Art & Design, Design & Technology, Geography, History, Media, Music, PE, Personal Social Health and Economic Education (PSHEE), Business, Science and a Modern Foreign Language.

(**Note:** Only students passing the 11+ are given the option to attend a Grammar school)

You need to focus on Mathematics, English, Science (Physics & Chemistry), IT or ICT, Design & Technology, Media, a research subject like history or geography, and a language.

SAT assessment continues in secondary education and is used to determine which GCSE class/level a pupil is placed when they take their options aged 14 years.

A pupil starts secondary education aged 12 years old.

Level 5 Average for a typical 13 years old,

Level 6 Average for a typical 14 years old,

Level 7 Above average for a typical 14 years old,

Level 8 Only available in mathematics.

The rating of A, B & C are applied to each level representing the child's progress in a level with A being the highest and C the lowest.

GCSE & EBAC

The General Certificate of Secondary Education (GCSE) is a qualifications based on individual subjects with the pupil generally taking a number of subjects in the English language curriculum, concluding with a final exam. The pupils study multiple subjects and complete course work, which is then marked by their teachers and contributes to their final examination grade. Taken over two years by students aged 14-16 years the GCSE is studied in England, Wales and Northern Ireland.

The English Baccalaureate (EBac) is not a qualification in itself. It is a recognition that a pupil in secondary education has achieved A* to C in GCSEs grades across a core of academic subjects – English, mathematics, history or geography, the sciences and a foreign language.

You are planning to go on to higher education and gain A Levels or BTEC qualifications.

You need to target a minimum of 44 points from your best 8 GCSE subjects, but you must verify the points required depending on your chosen sixth form college and course because some courses require a minimum point score in given GCSE's. Even if you score the points target but fail to score a specified grade for a particular subject you may not qualify for college. My advice is to work hard and get the grades, don't fail to achieve your dream at the first hurdle, study hard.

GCSE Point Scores

A* = 8 points = Distinction *

A = 7 points = Distinction

B = 6 points = Merit

C = 5 points = Pass

D = 4 points

E = 3 points

F = 2 points

IGCSE & CIE - COMPARABLE INTERNATIONAL SECONDARY SCHOOL EDUCATION

The International General Certificate of Secondary Education (IGCSE) is an exam based qualification equivalent to a GCSE and is based on the GCE O-Level for pupils whose first language may not be English. The IGCSE is intended to prepare a pupil for International Baccalaureate and Cambridge International Examination (CIE) CIE A-level.

IGCSE candidates include a first language, second language, mathematics and one or more subjects in the sciences. IGCSE candidates then choose additional courses and sit exams for the core and extended papers. The IGCSE is recognised by institutes and employers around the world as comparable to many international secondary school curricula.

The Cambridge IGCSE papers cover in excess of 70 subjects and these are being taken by students in over 120 countries worldwide, including the United States, Canada, Belgium, Spain, Italy, Malaysia, India, Bahrain, to name a few, you should check with your secondary school your IGCSE options.

F1 IN SCHOOLS

You will need to discuss with your school the merits of the F1 in Schools Project. This is a great experience, covering all the basic principle subjects of F1 car design covered in a fun programme.

The idea of the project is to inspire the next generation of engineers. All of the details you need whether you are a student, a teacher or would like to sponsor a school or the programme are available at **F1 In Schools**. Taking part in F1 in Schools is exactly the kind of extra curricula activity that would help you to stand out from the crowd of applicants that submit a CV to a Formula 1 team.

F1 in Schools is a not-for-profit multi-disciplinary challenge in which teams of students aged 9 to 19 use CAD/CAM software to collaborate, design, analyse, manufacture, test, and then race miniature gas powered balsa wood F1 cars. The finals are held all over the world so you get to experience travelling with your team and take part in the race.

FORMULA SCHOOLS

Formula Schools is an initiative to design a 1/18 scale radio-controlled car. Many schools now use the scheme to deliver courses such as GCSE in engineering, and the students learn about composites and material systems, electronics, bodywork & aerodynamics, powertrain and chassis design, team working and driving.

The learning can form part of the requirements of the KS4 curriculum.

For further details visit: **Formula Schools**.

If your school is not currently participating ask your teachers to introduce the initiative. Be the driver to make it happen.

IET FORMULA 24

Aimed at secondary schools or youth organisations for ages 11-16 years. This is a green power event. Other than the electric motor and batteries you are free to design the rest of the car as long as you conform to the regulations. Local & national events take place, several members of the team must drive the car and pit stops are required.

IET FORMULA 24+

Is aimed at 16-25 years A Level & University Students. Details for the IET 24 & 24+ can be found at **Greenpower Formula 24**.

JOHNNIE WALKER
BOSS
Mobil 1
BOSS HUGO BOSS
video
vodafone
MERCEDES
VODAFONE

6. SIXTH FORM SCHOOL & COLLEGE

GCE A LEVELS

Studied in a Sixth Form College or a Secondary Education Institute the General Certificate of Education Advanced Level, generally termed the A-level it is the GCE Advanced Level. It is an academic qualification offered to students completing secondary or pre-university education. The A-level subjects are studied over a two-year period with an examination test at the end of each year, AS in year 1 and A2 in year respectively. Most students study four A-level subjects simultaneously during Year 12, then drop one subject in Year 13 to focus on the three best subjects (ages 16–18).

Although the exam for AS is taken at the end of the 1st year it is not an A Level, it is a half A Level called an AS.

You have to have completed an AS and achieved a satisfactory grade to progress to the A2 course.

So what is the point of an AS qualification? Some students may choose to take 4 A level subjects and continue with them if they have not yet decided their career discipline. Although to attempt 4 A Level courses in a single year is a tough challenge. After the first year of study they will have a better idea of what they enjoy and what they wish to take to A2 level and cease to continue one subject and focus on getting the best grades from 3 A levels instead of 4 lower grade A Levels. However the AS is not a wasted qualification, some of the better and particularly academically focused Universities may request 3.5 A levels for certain subjects.

The A-Level is used to assess a student's suitability of application for entry to a University and admissions offers are considered based on a student's predicted A-level grades. The student is then expected to achieve the predicted grades. Failure to achieve your grades may result in the offer being withdrawn.

A Level Grading

A – top 10%

B – next 15%

C – next 10% - You must achieve a minimum C Grade in all subjects.

D – next 15%

E – next 20%

O (Ordinary) Level Grade

O - next 20%

Fail – final 10%

Total 100%

Candidates who did not achieve an A level grade of A-E are awarded an Ordinary Level Pass which indicated a performance equivalent to at least a grade C at GCE Ordinary Level. Please do not be that person. The cost of an A Level course can be in the region of £350; if you have to repeat your course this not only hurts your progress but it hits your pocket to add insult.

BTEC
BUSINESS AND TECHNOLOGY EDUCATION COUNCIL

BTEC takes a practical approach to learning, without missing any of the important theory of the subject. BTEC qualifications are a vocational course and are now taken in more than 100 countries. They range from Pre-GCSE education to a Degree equivalent and are governed by the Edexcel Foundation.

A BTEC Certificate is awarded as a Pass or Fail, which is not necessarily fair on a student that excelled to a student that just about qualified; the BTEC consists of 16 modules to make up one BTEC qualification. Each BTEC module is graded with the classifications of Pass, Merit and Distinction, and these are listed on a separate certificate to your diploma.

If a student wishes to demonstrate that they have excellent

credentials they should make sure they are able to state the quality of their BTEC Pass.

A single BTEC ND level 3 qualification is equivalent to 3x A levels and is extremely reputable.

If you are trying to gauge how an A level compares to a BTEC:

3x A Level A Grades = 1x BTEC Distinction Overall

3x A Level C Grades = 1x BTEC Merit Overall

3x A Level E Grades = 1x BTEC Pass Overall

A full list of BTEC courses can be found at: **EDEXCEL** but we recommend courses in:

BTEC Course In Engineering

BTEC Course In Mathematics

BTEC Course In ICT

BTEC Course In Science

BTEC Course Design & Technology

BTEC Course In Team Leading & Management

HIGHER EDUCATION

If you are looking at higher educational courses you should already have formed an idea of where your strengths lay and the direction of your chosen career.

F1 is more than just racing and engineering, and courses that are relevant to the modern F1 team and industry are:

- Mathematics,
- Engineering (General),
- Electrical & Electronics,
- Mechanical Engineering,

- Chemical Engineering,
- Instrumentation & Control,
- Process Engineering,
- Software Development,
- 3D Design & Model Making,
- Civil Engineering,
- Telecommunication,
- Marketing,
- Hospitality Management,
- Advertising & Public Relations,
- Fitness Health & Exercise,
- Applied Sports Science,
- Practical Journalism,
- Photography,
- Radio,
- Television,
- Accountancy & Finance, Law.

All of these courses can be pursued but there are also a number of jobs in formula one that do not require a diploma and they are equally as valuable to the effort of the teams. These are all listed later in the book.

Higher National Certificate HNC

A HNC is a level 4 course studied over 1 year full-time or 2 years as a part time course. It is equivalent to 1 year of University and a Certificate of Higher Education.

Certificate of Higher Education CertHE & International CertHE

The CertHE is the academic equivalent of a HNC and is a level 4 course, studied over 1 year or 2 years as a part time course. Holding a CertHE may in some cases reduce the period of time required to attain a Bachelor's degree by replacing some of the modules.

Higher National Diploma HND & International HND

A HND is a level 5 course. HND courses are available in automotive, motorsport, and engineering. An Engineering HND is a two years course and will teach you the fundamentals of engineering. If you have previously studied a HNC you may be able to complete a HND in 1 year.

An example of Mechanical HND course modules in year one are:

- Design & Materials,
- Engineering & mechanical Principles,
- Technology, Mathematics and Electronics & Computing,
- Introduction To Aerospace Engineering,
- Engineering Application & Practice (within the automotive and mechanical sectors).

The second year would comprise of a project and industrial placement, you would also study:

- Analytical Techniques,
- Electronics & Control,
- Design Method & Materials,
- Aerospace Engineering,
- Automotive Systems Engineering,
- Solid Mechanics & Thermo Fluids.

Diplomas of Higher Education DipHE & International DipHE

A Diploma of Higher Education is a Level 5 course. This is the academic equivalent of the vocational HND course. You may find that the programme of study is the same or similar to a foundation degree.

Attending a University is not the only choice open to you; the Open University also offers a number of the recommended courses and we cover this later in the book.

7. UNIVERSITY EDUCATION

There are several degrees to study building on the higher education courses, and to explain the full content and diversity of every course would result in an encyclopedia. The following explanation of degrees has been based on becoming an engineer in the race team or design office, and outlines the level of depth of the subject that you would be expected to learn and attainment required on any course. References to Civil Engineering are with race track and facility design in mind.

UNIVERSITY APPLICATION

All undergraduate applications need to be made through the Universities and Colleges Admissions Service; you should visit **UCAS** for further information on the application requirements.

Applying for a course does not constitute full acceptance from the University. The University will make an offer based on predicted grades. This is called a Conditional Offer of Acceptance. If you do not achieve the grades the University reserve the right to withdraw the offer or you may be asked to attend an interview to explain any exceptional circumstance that may have affected your grade.

UNIVERSITY LEVELS OF EDUCATION

Undergraduate

Undergraduate education is post-secondary school education and includes Foundation degree's, Honour's degree and up to the level of Bachelor's degree in the UK, such as in the United States, where a university entry level is known as undergraduate, while students of higher degrees are known as graduates. In some other educational systems and subjects, undergraduate education is post-secondary education up to the level of a master's degree, for example in some science courses in Britain and courses in Europe.

Post Graduate

A Bachelor's degree or a first in other professional qualifications or an academic certificate is required to study Post-graduate education (or graduate education in North America). Post Graduate education is normally considered to be part of higher education. In North America, this level is generally referred to as graduate school.

Graduate

It is a requirement that a student has previously earned an Undergraduate Bachelor's degree to study at this level. A graduate school awards advanced academic Master's degree or Doctoral PhD. A distinction is typically made between graduate schools (where courses of study do not provide training for a particular profession) and professional schools, which offer specialised advanced degrees in professional fields such as business, engineering, ministry or law.

TYPES OF DEGREE

An academic degree is a college or university diploma associated to either a title or an academic position which is awarded in recognition of the recipient having either satisfactorily completed a prescribed course of study, or having conducted a scholarly endeavour deemed worthy of admission to the degree.

A University credit is the equivalent of 10 notional study hours. Each module is a self-contained part of the programme of study and carries a credit rating. The duration of all the study programme may be extended by one year through enrolment on the Engineering Foundation Year.

Balance of Study

When choosing your courses you need to ensure that you are not focusing to heavily on a single topic, for an engineer we would recommend developing a series of skills and you should ask your university the balance of the course they propose.

As a guide to the balance of studies required is as follows:

- 50% Mechanical, Electrical & Engineering Science
- 20% Engineering Design & Manufacturing
- 18% Engineering Mathematics
- 12% Management & Professional Skills

Degree Grading

Degrees can be awarded with and without Honours, and degree classifications are not rigidly fixed. Some discretion is allowed for University Officials to have a small range of discretion to award and Honours based on the students continued effort and achievements as well as any final exam.

1. First-class Honours (70% and above) - also known as a First or 1st (Hons)
    a. A double first is first in two subjects
2. Second-class Honours (50% - 70%) (Hons)
    a. Upper Second-Class Honours (60% to 70) – also known as a 2:1
    b. Lower Second-Class Honours – (50% to 60%) also known as 2:2
3. Third-class Honours (40% to 50%) – also known as a Third (Hons)
4. Ordinary Degree (35% to 39%) – also known as a Pass.
5. Honours Degree – This is a research academic degree based on a single year full time study or two years part time and is graded as being between an undergraduate and post-graduate qualification. This award is based on an undergraduate students average grade over the course.

Note: It is important to recognise that a degree with (Hons) is not to be confused with an honours degree; they are different achievements.

You need to check with your chosen University the credit score between an ordinary degree and a degree with honours. As a guide a BA/BSc requires that you undertake at least 300 credits across the 3 years and pass at least 240 of them so you can have a BA or BSc.

Ordinary Degree of Bachelor of Engineering BEng (Ordinary) requires the successful completion of at least 300 credit points, including 60 points at Honours level.

If you wish to achieve your BA/BSc with Honours you need to achieve a grade of 120 points per year. Therefore a BEng (Hons) will require the successful attainment of 360 points.

Foundation Degree (FdEng, FdSc)

A Foundation Degree is a Level 5 course, and takes two years to complete and requires a minimum of 240 credits. Because Foundation Degrees are designed in partnership with employers it will help you gain technical and professional skills that employers demand. The practical skills and academic knowledge that you learn during the course will be valuable in your career. This qualification combines the study of engineering fundamentals like energy, design, manufacturing, materials, mechanics and structural analysis, mathematics and the study of real-life problems, entrepreneurship, work-related issues such as health and safety and project management. This in turn makes you much more employable and will help you climb the ladder once you have graduated.

Your future employers will know that that you have developed your work skills, have practical experience and the capability to progress to graduate level employment or Honours Degree paving the way to many new career opportunities.

If you're working in engineering-related employment at a technical level a foundation degree is for you. The Foundation Degree in Engineering is considered a step up from an apprenticeship. It also provides a route to an Honours degree in engineering.

There are specialised courses to consider, like a Foundation Degree in Materials Fabrication and Engineering that brings together qualifications offered by The Welding Institute (TWI) the world centre for materials joining technology, with engineering and mathematics modules. The Open University offers a number of these courses.

Honours Degrees

An Honours Degrees is a level 5 course and requires the attainment of 240 credits. They are offered in a number of vocational subjects and aim to provide graduates with the ability to investigate and think independently, research and innovate. Graduates will develop a comprehensive practical knowledge and understanding of their chosen discipline, elements of which will be at the forefront of research and current academic thinking. Employers require graduates who can analyse current practices and processes, evaluate evidence and then use sound judgment to make decisions, often in complex and unpredictable circumstances.

An Honours degree is a postgraduate qualification that includes an additional year of study after the bachelor's degree in the discipline of your choice. To qualify for an Honours degree, you are required to have prior high academic performance in undergraduate degree study.

If you have already studied a Foundation Degree or a Higher National Diploma and would like to gain an Honours Degree, in your final year you could opt to study a BA/BSc (Hons) or a bespoke one-year top-up option.

Bachelors Degree

A Bachelors Degree is a level 6 course and requires the attainment of 300-360 credits. Most higher education institutions generally offer certificates and several programmes leading to the attainment of a Master of Advanced Studies and Chartered Engineer status.

The Bachelor's Degree provides a solid base of transferable skills as well as engineering science core skills. You will study the process of design, working with others, how to combine design and innovation, with engineering design and computational modules. This is not just an academic course; principles are also practiced within the second year Industrial Based Design Project. The application of engineering science and the solution of industrial problems is a strong theme throughout Bachelor and Masters courses.

You can study either an Open BA/BSc or chose a discipline to study like a BEng (Hons)

Open BA/BSc Degree

The BA/BSc Open is one of the most flexible undergraduate programmes. A BSc requires a minimum of 300 credits and a BA requires a minimum of 360 credits. It is a two years course and is highly regarded by employers for its breadth of subjects and valued by students for the flexibility of courses to study. With this degree you have the freedom and opportunity to achieve a uniquely tailored qualification to match your specific job ambition.

You can study any subjects you like, in any combination, enabling you to chose one main discipline and then have the flexibility to mix in other modules to make up your credits. You will develop a wide range of expertise, skills and capabilities that are greatly sought after in today's highly competitive job market.

Specific BA/BSc – (BEng), (BSc), (BPhys), (BTech)

It is the study of a chosen discipline like engineering and requires a minimum of 360 credits, the BEng (Hons) also fully satisfies the educational requirements for Incorporated Engineer (IEng). The BEng is a thorough general engineering degree course and is IMechE accredited to many Universities. It explores the fundamentals of this creative and analytical subject through theoretical and practical application study based on real industrial practices. It covers the range of techniques, concepts and knowledge required by professional engineers. You will also be teamed up with other students to work on projects with the aim of building your teamwork and leadership skills and to create innovative solutions to challenging problems.

The learning outcomes fulfil the Engineering Council's requirements under UK-SPEC, and the course includes personal career planning to help you fulfill your professional aims.

A BEng is a firm foundation on which to build a successful career.

Years 1 and 2 Course Structure BEng Mechanical Engineering:

- Application of Engineering
- Design Control Engineering
- Electronics and Electrical Technology
- Engineering Computation
- Engineering Dynamics

- Engineering Mechanics
- Engineering Management
- Heat Transfer and Fluid Flow
- Industry Based Project
- Materials and Manufacturing Processes
- Mathematics
- Mechanics of Materials
- Thermodynamics
- Environmental Techniques
- Energy & Sustainability

Courses to consider:

BEng (Hons) Mechanical Engineer

BEng (Hons) Engineering (Mechanical) (Part-Time)

BEng (Hons) Aeronautics & Astronautics

BEng (Hons) Automotive Engineering

BSc (Hons) Mathematics

BSc (Hons) Software Development

BEng (Hons) Materials Engineering

BEng (Hons) Electrical Engineering

BEng (Hons) Electrical & Electronic Engineering

BEng (Hons) Mechatronics Engineering

BEng (Hons) Civil Engineering

BEng (Hons) Computer Engineering Degree

BA/BSc (Hons) Degree in Design & Innovation

Note: that a Honours degree is a 3 years course in many Universities, and that a Bachelors Degree is required if you wish to progress to a Master Degree.

Masters Degree (MEng), (MChem), (MPhys)

MEng Overview

The Masters Degree is a level 7 course and requires the attainment of 480 credits. The MEng requires 4 years of study with the course covering lectures, laboratory work, coursework and exams and is intended to give you a substantial technical depth of knowledge in a breadth of disciplines while acting in the role of Mechanical Engineer in the industrial context. The aim of the course is to continue to develop core engineering practices, and developing your skills of communication and leadership, over and beyond that of the BEng course.

The third and fourth academic years provide an opportunity to study your chosen specialist subjects in depth. In addition, MEng students are offered the chance to study a European language and follow extra courses in practical business management, design and micro-processor control systems.

During the fourth academic year, MEng students from different degree courses are brought together in multi-disciplinary teams to solve challenging industrially based problems at a number of different companies on a range of year-long projects.

Years 3 and 4 Compulsory modules:

- Project Leadership
- Project Engineering
- New Product Design
- Mechatronics
- Computer Control and Instrumentation
- Engineering Design Management
- Individual Project
- Group Design Project

Optional subjects:

The following examples of optional subjects support the BEng and MEng courses:

- Stress Analysis
- Structural Integrity
- Materials Engineering
- Materials Processing
- Laser Materials Processing
- Vibration, Noise and Rotordynamics
- Advanced Heat Transfer
- Computer Aided Design
- Computational Fluid Dynamics
- Contact Mechanics: Tribology
- Design for Assembly
- Design of Machinery
- Digital Image Processing
- Finite Element Analysis
- Internal Combustion Engines
- Languages
- Laser Optical Measurements
- Metrology
- Rapid Prototyping
- Robotics and Control
- Sports Engineering
- Healthcare Engineering
- Turbomachinery

Cambridge University offers a specialist graduate degree in Aerospace & Aerothermal Engineering that is a blend of many subjects.

MSc Aerospace & Aerothermal Overview

The Third Year of Core Study would include:

- Fluid Mechanics - 4 module
- Heat & Mass Transfer
- Thermodynamics & Power Generation

You would also study two of the following Companion Modules in your third year:

- Mathematical Methods
- Mechanics of Solids
- Systems & Controls
- Radio Frequency Electronics
- Signals & Systems
- Integrated Digital Electronics
- Materials Processing & Design
- Dynamics
- Vibration
- Fracture Mechanics of Material Structures
- Structural Materials and Design
- Structural Analysis and Stability
- Finite Element Methods

The forth year would include the core subjects of:

- Aerodynamics
- Computational Fluid Dynamics

- Molecular Dynamics
- Flow Instability
- Aeroacoustics
- Turbomachinery
- Aircraft Stability & Control
- Turbulence & Vortex Dynamics

You would also study two of the following Companion Modules in your forth year:

- Design Methods
- Designing with Composites
- Design Case Studies
- Advanced Linear Vibration
- Random and Non-Linear Vibrations
- Continuum Mechanics
- Control System Design
- Electronic Sensors & Instrumentation
- MEMS: Design (MicroElectroMechanical Systems)
- Robust and Non-Linear Systems & Control
- Optimal & Predictive Control

MSc in Aeronautics Overview

An MSc in Aeronautic is a 1 year course and covers advanced computational methods and would cover the following modules.

- Fundamentals of fluid mechanics
- Flow management
- Fluid Structure Interaction
- Finite difference methods

- Finite element method
- Advanced Flight Mechanics
- Aeroelasticity and fluid-structure interaction
- Analysis of Laminated Composites
- Compressible flow
- Control theory
- Experimental fluid dynamics
- Hydrodynamic stability
- Linear algebra
- Navier-Stokes equations and turbulence modelling
- Separated flows and fluid-structure interaction
- Structural dynamics
- Technology of sensors and actuators

MSc Electrical Power Systems Engineering Overview

Gives you a broad knowledge and sound understanding in electrical power engineering and the skills you need to make good decisions based on solid foundations of the principles. Gives an in depth knowledge into issues and problems faced by electrical power engineers and the techniques used to solve these problems.

- Project Management
- New and Renewable Energy Systems
- Electrical Power Systems and Electrical Propulsion
- Electrical Machines and Power Electronic Drives
- Power Transmission and Auxiliary Machinery Systems
- Group Project

Gaining a MEng or MSC is the best route to chartered status.

PhD Doctorate

PhD, Eng.D (Engineering), D.Sc Doctor of Science, D.B.A Doctor of Business Administration, D.Prof/ProfD Professional Doctorate

A PhD Doctorate is a level 8 course. This is the highest academic degree that a student can attain. The main criteria for a PhD is to demonstrate that you have mastered the chosen subject completely by writing a dissertation (also known as a thesis). A dissertation requires the demonstration of your intellectual knowledge through exploring, investigating and thinking about everything you have read or studied, and through additional research helping to expand your knowledge about the subject of your study.

On top of this you will have to go through an oral examination on the thesis you have submitted to prove that you created the work. Occasionally you may also be required to undertake other tests as the examiners may decide.

On the successful completion and award you will be able to use the title of Doctor.

THE COST OF HIGHER EDUCATION

The cost of higher education does vary by course, by country and by institution. Any price indicated is only intended as a guide at the time of publishing and would need to be independently confirmed by you as you choose your course and university. You would also need to consider the currency exchange fees.

The figures indicated will appear to be very daunting to anyone, but what you have to consider is that you are making an investment in your future, the better qualified you are the higher the position in a company you can achieve and earn a higher salary, or charge higher fees for your services. So your potential to repay the investment increases with each grade and qualification. There is also financial help offered in the means of a student loan and living costs loan, so you can be assured funding is available but it is down to you to make the application and agree the terms of repayment.

Higher Education

1. For a BTEC Level 3 course the cost could be in the region of £350-£500
2. A HNC or HND Level 4 course studied full-time per year could be in the region of £1,100-£1,350 per course.

Note: It is your responsibility to check the fees for your chosen course.

University Fees

Recent changes to the UK fees now mean that a University can charge up to £9000 per year.

- An Undergraduates Level 5 course & Post Graduate Degree Level 6 course studied full-time per year ranges from £3500 to £9000, so the cost of your two years course would be in the range of £7000 to £18,000. If you chose to add the third year for your honours degree, add the cost of another years education
- The overall cost to add a Masters Degree could cost another £18,000.
- PhD (full-time) UK/EU students (per annum): £18,000-£21,000
- PhD (part-time) UK/EU students (per annum): £9,000-£11,000

You may be able to get a student loan to assist you through your academic years, at PhD level sponsorship from a company or organisation may also be available, but you would need to check this independently with the University and sponsor. Note that you do not need to start repaying the loan until you have graduated and are earning in excess of £21,000.

For a summary of fees visit: **The Complete University Guide**

For advice on managing your costs accrued as a student visit: **Save The Student**

You could look to the **GOV.UK Education & Learning** website for further information, or check with your chosen education institute administration department for advice.

UNIVERSITY ENTRY REQUIREMENTS

General Entrance Requirements

Each University determines its own entry requirements so you need to be clear on their expectations and it is a good idea to look at the preferred University courses during your school years when you are considering your options or sixth form courses. Fortunately there is a wide range of qualifications for entry but please remember the following is a guide and you need to check with your chosen University the course entry requirements. As well as achieving your grades, you may be required to attend an interview or complete an admission test.

If you do not meet the General Entrance requirement, most universities have caveats to enable them to admit good students with complex backgrounds. Just like any advantage wishing to be gained in F1, you should always make sure you know the rules and caveats if you think you may struggle to meet all of your grades, this could be useful during your application or interview process to help you secure a place at University.

English Language Requirements (UK) (GCSE)

Students must meet the minimum of a GCE or GCSE pass in English Language Grade C or above.

International GCSE (IGCSE)

English as a First Language attaining IGCSE Level 2 Certificate Grade C.

International English Language

International English Language Testing System (IELTS) score of 6.5 or an equivalent qualification.

A-Levels

You will be expected to offer at least three full GCE A-Levels, or replace one with a Critical Thinking A-Level. You may be able to draw on a caveat and replace one of your A-Levels with two subjects at GCE AS-Level. General Studies is not usually accepted as one of your three A-Levels

International Baccalaureate Diploma

To qualify for a UK University you need to have attained Grade 4 in the English language, and have successfully studied three subjects at a Higher Level to attain a full International Baccalaureate Diploma, scoring 38-40 points and 6's & 7's in the higher level subjects.

BTEC Higher National Certificate & Higher National Diploma (HNC/HND)

For BTEC HNC & HND the minimum acceptable is a level 5 Pass in which you should achieve a minimum of 5 merits (one of which is math) from 16 units studied, in some cases this may allow applicants to progress directly to year two of the course where previous study fits with the chosen course. In some cases an A Level may be required with a BTEC qualification to make up 18 units studied for some courses.

Diploma of Higher Education (DipHE) & Advanced Diploma

You will need 15 credits at level two and 45 credits at level three. You may also need to meet minimum GCSE grade C and in some cases Grade B GCSE, or A Level for certain courses.

The Open University (OU) Openplus

The Open University is a partner in the OpenPlus scheme with many Universities, and offers courses in Science based subjects. If you have already successfully completed a two years course you may be able to progress directly to the second year of a full BSc degree.

For further details visit: **The OU Openplus**

Extended Project

Although an extended project is not usually accepted as a qualification on your application, it may be looked upon as favorable against another student's application, so you should make the effort to note the achievement on your application.

If you have any questions on how your qualifications compare to the UK visit: **NARIC**. The significance of comparing your qualification to the UK is that many teams are based in the UK, as a clear comparison is the perfect way to state your F1 pedigree. It also works for any UK based engineers if they wish to work for a team based in Europe.

UNIVERSITY INTERVIEW

You need to submit an application to UCAS, to be invited to an interview and subsequently to join the University. You will attend the University and be given a tour of the facilities and asked questions in relation to your career ambitions so that the lecturers can determine if the course applied for is in line with your career ambition, and that you are serious about the effort required to achieve your academic target. They will also check that you have the appropriate entry requirements. If you do not have the required entry requirements you will need to be able to state why they should consider you as suitable for the course and prepare a supporting letter for the lecturer.

It is important that the University does not give out places on the courses too easily because spaces are limited and they have to make tough choices to narrow the prospective students to those with the desire, ambition and capability to contribute constructively to the course and complete the modules.

Do not attend with the intention of "winging it". A great career is formed out of preparation and hard work. Make sure that you write down your ambition and explain how the course would put you on the right career path. Rehearse your answers, prepare notes in advance and refer to notes if required during the interview. If you need to use notes explain to the interviewer that the opportunity means so much that you have written notes so that you do not forget to mention anything.

You also need to ask the interviewer what they will do for you, and ask about any details you are not sure of. The interview is a two way dialogue, you need to be sure that it is right University for you as well as the University making sure you are the right student.

It is essential that you ask about support offered to students, you may be eligible for financial support and assistance with accommodation.

Please remember that student accommodation needs to be applied for separately, it is not given as a result of joining the course. You need to apply and this can take a number of weeks to be confirmed. My advice is to apply sooner rather than later and the University can provide you with the application details.

PREFERRED UNIVERSITIES

There are preferred Universities where graduates are favoured, these are Brunel, Bristol, Cambridge, Imperial, Loughborough, Oxford Brookes, Cranfield and Southampton being popular traditional choices for F1 hopefuls and the F1 teams.

Engineering Disciplines

- **Brunel School of Engineering and Design – Uxbridge West London UK.**
- **Faculty of Engineering - Bristol UK.**
- **Department of Engineering – Cambridge UK.**
- **Faculty of Engineering – Imperial - South Kensington London UK.**
- **Faculty of Engineering – Loughborough Leicestershire UK.**
- **Faculty of Engineering – Southampton UK.**
- **Department of Mechanical Engineering & Mathematical Sciences – Oxford UK.**
- **Advanced Motorsport Engineering - Cranfield UK.**

Aeronautical & Aerospace Engineering

- **Brunel School of Engineering and Design – Uxbridge West London UK. Aerospace**
- **Faculty of Engineering - Bristol UK. Aerospace**
- **Department of Engineering – Cambridge UK. Aerospace & Aerothermal Engineering**

- **Faculty of Engineering – South Kensington London UK. Department of Aeronautics**
- **Faculty of Engineering – Loughborough Leicestershire UK. Aeronautical Engineering**
- **Faculty of Engineering – Southampton UK. – Aeronautics & Astronautics**

You should also look seriously at University Technical Colleges, for example you have the UTC Silverstone in the UK that opened in September 2013. The UTC at Silverstone has a distinct advantage over many of the traditional Universities in that it is based at a circuit with multiple motorsport teams and suppliers based on its door-step. This is a good opportunity for students to visit and learn from experienced race engineers. Being based at a circuit you could prove in practice your design and ideas, and shakedown your vehicle. Theory is a good basis but practical experience is irreplace-able.

The courses focus at GCSE Level for ages 14-16 covering the core subjects of math, science, English, German, media & IT, PE and geography. You can move onto a higher education Baccalaureate Diplomas for ages 16-18 years and cover business and technical events management & high performance engineering.

Visit **UTC Silverstone** for further details.

Links to all of these Universities are provided in the members area of the **www.jobsinf1.com** website.

FORMULA STUDENT

Many of these colleges and Universities participate in an event called Formula Student, and this is the complete design of vehicle systems including the development of electric and hybrid vehicle systems. The students are expected to design, build, prepare and test their vehicle prior to participating in events with other colleges and universities.

Colleges and universities compete from all over Europe, so there is a lot of kudos involved in succeeding and performing well in this event. It is important that the students recognise just what an achievement it is even to participate, let alone to win or be podium placed in this event, and it's a key point that every student should put on their CV.

Formula student is the testing ground for future F1 engineers, for further details of how to get involved visit: **Formula Student.**

THE OPEN UNIVERSITY

If you are a non UK resident or you have already finished your formal education and are now working for a living it is tough to make the decision to return to full time education. The choice open to you is to consider an Open University course to gain a UK based education. There are several modules to be studied and the full course will take approximately 6 years to complete. You have a maximum of 12 years in which to complete and graduate. The commitment required is approximately 12-16 hours a week depending on the module being studied.

A BEng (Bachelor of Engineering) will give you a solid foundation, and you could also consider specialised short courses to top up an existing education. An MEng (Master Engineering) will put you on a level playing field with many of your fellow professionals. You may choose to continue to a CEng (Chartered Engineer) degree or progress to a PhD (Doctor of Philosophy).

A good place to start is The Open University to determine the right course for you. A University Degree can be very rewarding especially if you become a Chartered or Incorporated Engineer. Professionally qualified engineers now rank among the highest paid professionals, this is because many countries now have a shortage of engineers as many people choose careers in IT and services. You should consider the following choices of engineering degree and qualification.

The OU's BEng (Hons) (B65) and the MEng (M03) have been accredited by the Institution of Engineering and Technology (IET) and the Institution of Mechanical Engineers (IMechE). You should also consider membership of the Society of Automotive Engineers (SAE). A specialised organisation is the Royal Aeronautical Society (RAeS). These are great institutions and a terrific source of information and offer a means to mix with fellow professionals.

OU Engineering Degree Courses

- Foundation Degree In Engineering
- Foundation Degree in Materials Fabrication and Engineering
- BA/BSc Open degree
- BA/BSc (Honours) Design and Innovation
- BEng Bachelor of Engineering (Honours)
- MEng Masters Degree of Engineering

The Open University does change its courses from time to time but a good indication of the amount of work you will need to do and the courses to study are:

Stage 1

T174 Engineering The Future

- Block1 Contexts, Conquests and Consequences
- Block 2 Engineering By Design
- Block 3 Engineering To Rule parts 1-5
- Block 4 Engineering For Products parts 1-3
- Block 5 Pushing Back The Boundaries parts 1-2
- T176 Engineering: professions, practice and skills 1
- MST121 Mathematics & MS221 Exploring Mathematics or
- MST124 Essential Mathematics 1 & MST125 Essential Mathematics
- S151 Maths for Science

Stage 2

T207 Engineering: Mechanics, Materials, Design

- Block 1 Problems Challenges & Opportunities parts 1-2
- Block 2 Static Structures: Shelter & Protection parts 1-4
- Block 3 Dynamics: Getting Moving parts 1-4
- Block 4 Resources: Fluids & Energy parts 1-3
- Block 5 Endurance: Improving Performance parts 1-5
- Block 5 Fail Safe
- Block 6 Human Factors parts 1-2

T211 Design & Designing

T218 Design For Engineers

T276 Engineering: professions, practice and skills 2

Stage 3

T307 Innovation: designing for a sustainable future

- Block 1 Introduction To A Sustainable Future
- Block 2 Markets
- Block 3 Products
- Block 4 Diffusion
- Block 5 Consumption

T357 Structural integrity: designing against failure

- Block 1 Fracture mechanics
- Block 2 Failure modes
- Block 3 Environmental factors

T397 Key Skills For Professional Engineers

T450 The Engineering Project – To Complete Your Degree

T398 Towards Chartership: professional development for engineers.

All of the courses mentioned offer a good foundation in engineering to support a career in F1, but if your dream is in any other role in F1 you need to research the disciplines of the subject, the colleges, universities and the entry requirements.

There are also a number of jobs in Formula 1 that do not require a degree and they are equally as valuable to the effort of the teams. These are listed later in the book.

8. CREATING A GREAT CV

When you write a CV you need to be fully aware that it is not just a case of writing down your professional credentials but also that you need to format your CV for both human and electronic assessment.

In the modern recruitment world agencies and F1 teams use search engines and electronic "bots" to read a page on the internet and assess the relevance of the CV to the exact language and words used by the person that created the search.

Both will look to assess your objective, and an example of this is to state for example "Seeking a role as an aerodynamic senior engineer".

A recruiter that is in possession of your CV whether in paper or electronic copy will read the whole sentence to assess the relevance, but will also make a conscious interpretation if your CV stated "an experienced aerodynamics engineer" as to its relevance to an aerodynamic senior engineer role they wish to fill.

A bot will make an assessment of each word used in the search, the sequence, the exact spelling and the exact wording used in the writing of your CV. So the recruiter would have to write the exact wording used on your CV for you to appear as relevant to the bots search programme when it is trawling the through the internet for applicants.

The challenge you face is that a recruiter will use the internet to find a CV in the first instance unless anyone else working at the company is able to put a CV on the table in front of them, or if they already have a CV registered with the company.

So we are talking about search engine optimisation (SEO) of your CV if you are going to stand any chance of being found. It is not possible to write a professional looking CV with all permutations of your skill descriptions, so we need to consider "Keywords" to use. But keyword listing is not enough, search engines are getting smarter and context and relevance algorithms are being developed.

Each section of your CV must meet the search criteria, from seeking a role, to education and experience and potentially personal interest.

So formatting a CV and using the correct layout expected is essential. Equally as important is the fact that a CV will be assessed in 7 to 15 seconds by any reader. If the layout and content do not jump off the page you are in the bin under the table.

Recruiters also have some golden rules when it comes to creating a CV. Number one on the list is only use two pages. This is easy if you are only starting out from University but if you are an experienced engineer two pages might not be enough. So you now have a dilemma to overcome. Pages verses content? The answer to this is high quality content on two pages.

While you may use a vocabulary in your industry how do you know a recruiter will use the same keyword phrasing? Most recruitment personnel will not have an engineering or motorsport background, this is by no means a criticism they are very good at their job, but an engineer or designer thinks differently to a person in an administrative role and you CV needs to match their search criteria.

Jobs in F1 have a keyword relevance tool that works on all search engines to determine the statistically optimised phrases and keywords used by recruiters. We also have an optimised CV layout that shows you exactly what a recruiter expects to see in an easy to read format.

To access this information join the members area at:
www.jobsinf1.com.

9. APPRENTICESHIPS IN F1

Many people without a degree see an apprenticeship as their route into F1 and plan to start at the bottom and work their way up. This is a noble work ethic but what you have to appreciate is that those people working up the hierarchy are there through their own hard work and education, and without continuing to improve your education you may not have a long career in F1.

Very few teams actually take on an apprentice; the preference is always to find somebody that has a degree or specialises in a particular discipline. An apprenticeship programme lasts about four years, and as an example, a team may only actually take on five apprentices. So that is five people over the four years period, and they'll have approximately one hundred applicants for each of those positions.

So, if you were hoping that this would be your way into F1, the chances are very slim, not impossible, but you would have to have such a unique CV or way of presenting yourself. You would need to demonstrate a leadership or something that really attracts their attention into liking you as an individual. We explain later in the book how to do that little something extra. Your other route in is if you are related to someone working for the team and that is working for the team at the time of apprenticeship assessment to get your foot through the door.

Getting onto an apprenticeship scheme does not mean that you will be designing cars the next week, far from it. You will be doing the very basic of jobs required within the company: you will be fetching tools, cleaning tools, mopping the floor, loading trucks and being a general assistant to the team. The chances of you being allowed to work on an F1 car within your first six months to a year are fairly slim. You will have to demonstrate a good appreciation for the engineering and science behind preparing a vehicle before you will be allowed near one.

There are two recognised routes to an engineering apprenticeship in F1. The first is to ensure good GCSE grades at school and in particular math and sciences, as well as design and technology or vocational training in mechanics. A good education is a foundation that will provide the opportunity to go on to study an Apprenticeship, in conjunction with a HNC, or HND qualification, or alternatively A Levels. It will also help you to determine how successful you might be at completing these key subjects at a higher level of education.

The second is demonstrating your capability in the F1 in Schools and Formula schools initiatives, or gaining relevant work experience, part time jobs or related hobbies such as mechanics or karting will also help your chances of securing the limited opportunities.

You can also consider an Open University course. You should start this at the very outset of your apprenticeship, because it will take you 6 years to get a degree. A BEng (Bachelor of Engineering) degree will give you a good foundation for your F1 career, but be prepared to put in about 12-16 hours a week to study.

You can consider an apprenticeship outside of a Formula 1 team and then look to move to take a job in the manufacturing department of an F1 team. This is a good option for model makers, pattern makers, machine programmers, machinists and composite lay up personnel.

10. INTERSHIPS IN F1

An internship is a period of work offered by an employer to give students and graduates exposure to the working environment and experience of working in a field related to their studies. The period of Internships can range from a week or as long as a year. Before you start an internship it's important to know your rights with regards to getting paid.

Internships are not limited to engineering roles but also include all other company functions like marketing, graphic design, management, I.T to name a few. Your college or university should be able advise you on suitable schemes for your career.

Having working experience can be as valuable as anything learned in your studies. Internships are great opportunities to speak directly to people who have experience in the role you aspire to; and their knowledge of the job and working environment will give you a greater understanding of what job is all about. Throughout an internship you will develop a variety of soft skills, including communication skills, personal effectiveness, discipline, presentation skills, creative problem solving and influencing skills and learn to operate as part of team and learn to follow instruction.

Some teams offer an online application process and this is designed to check your intelligence and aptitude. The team are looking for personal characteristic traits that demonstrate intelligence, teamwork, perseverance, resourcefulness, and lateral thinking.

1. This consists of a series of puzzles and general knowledge about the team & drivers. Some basic mathematics and a test of your hand and eye co-ordination and memory.
2. You would need to complete an application form that will be judged on content & creativity.
3. You would then be asked to make a video interview and submit this to the team. Finally you will be asked to attend an interview.

In order to apply you need to contact the team headquarters and enquire if any internship is being offered for the coming season.

For a bit of fun you can try out your mental dexterity and have a go at the RedBull F1 Internship Challenge. This is an opportunity to prepare for questions that could be put to you in an interview.

11. USING SOCIAL MEDIA TO RAISE YOUR PROFILE & BUILD NETWORK

Today, there are many tools that you can use in social media to increase your visibility in the market place and enable you to communicate, and link with fellow professionals. In the past, it used to be very, very difficult to actually rub shoulders and shake hands with the people that were at the top of their profession, and what social media enables you to do is open the door, instead of spending many years trying to work your way up the ladder. It can put you straight in contact with the people that matter in the industry.

It is now more important than ever that any professional person has an online presence. And if you specialise in a particular discipline, you may choose to have your own website that explains the basis of your service, enabling you to sell and market yourself. There are also a multitude of tools that you may not have realised can put your career on the fast track if used properly.

FACEBOOK FOR BUSINESS

Jobs in F1 has a Facebook page, **Facebook/Jobsinf1**, and like any other social network, this is mainly used as a means to socialise with other people of similar interests in a fun and relaxed manner. By liking and sharing the page, you will join the other fans and the community of people working in F1 and be able to see their fun and interesting posts about what's going on at F1 headquarters, at the Grand Prix and in the pit lanes, the PR events occurring and really pick up little bits and pieces of information that you wouldn't ordinarily have access to.

You will be able see where people are in the world as they travel with the circus and upload their posts. Keep a log of who you find and initiate dialogue, they may become your friends, and as we all know sometimes it's not what you know, but whom you know that can get you a job.

You can use this as a means to ask technical questions or see technology explained by the PR team. You will likely see some great pictures, and it's a good medium for you to keep track of new jobs being posted without having to work too hard.

It's also a great place for you to upload pictures, or even do a video and put it on Facebook to tell us and potential employers who you are, what kind of education you have, and what sort of job you're looking for. This is a great and simple way to effectively do an interview without actually having to go through the process of applying and looking for the job, because getting a job can actually be quite easy, and what you need to do is to learn to use these social tools and let the rest of the world find you.

The **Facebook/Jobsinf1** page was created so that you have a means to stay in touch and not have your personal Facebook account flooded by F1 comments. Not all of your friends may be as passionate as you, so this is an ideal way to keep your worlds in a great place.

TWITTER

You need to use Twitter in a slightly different way to Facebook. We recommend if you do not have a Twitter account you should get one. During the F1 Grand Prix, several of the pit crew, the PR team will be posting on Twitter to the Sky Sports app, this is read by a huge audience and is an opportunity to interact and choose who to follow based on your career interest.

By looking at the Twitter feeds, you may be able to identify people's names within each of the F1 companies or peripheral industries, and Jobs in F1 has a strategy that will help you to find out who works for each team, and what their role and position is.

As an example if you are interested in being an F1 TV presenter then you can follow the presenters and ask them questions like who is your TV agent, you may want to ask who is the trucky and tyre man, and use this approach to build up your contacts. The guys in the garage are the unknown hero's so appeal to their ego, and ask them to post about their role in F1.

So, you may be able to develop a rapport with members of the teams, and build a relationship by communicating with them, or even if you have the opportunity, to meet them in a pit lane if you've bought yourself some pit lane passes.

LINKED IN

A very powerful social tool is LinkedIn as it enables you to put your profile online simply, and for prospective employers and agencies to be able to view your profile, and your CV. Depending on how you structure your CV and the content, this could be enough to get you headhunted.

A recruiter is able to see your employment history and skillset without needing a copy of your CV. Your former and current colleagues are able to endorse your skills and leave a testimonial that states for example, how professional and how good you are at your job, what a pleasure you are to work with and how dedicated you are.

You need to be selective which recruiters you allow into your network. It is easy to be overrun with unwanted job offers in business sectors that you have no interest in.

In LinkedIn, you can also join groups, and these are people with a common interest in a particular topic, for example, hybrid vehicle technology or ESS systems. Once you are accepted to a group, you can then add comments to the forum and open discussions with people. You can also start your own groups and start your own forums, and this will enable you to build up a network of people that specialise in a particular topic, you can not only share your knowledge and skill with them, but also use this as a means to promote your ability.

You can build your network of professionals in LinkedIn, by adding connections. What this means is that you can send an invite to other colleagues that you have worked with in the past, to people that are part of your group contacts or potential new contacts.

If people accept your invitations, then they become part of your LinkedIn network. And once you have built a network of friends and colleagues in LinkedIn, you can send messages like emails to and from each other to keep each other informed of what you're doing and your progress. This is also a useful means to network any kind of jobs or opportunities that may exist, or even just to ask people do they know anybody that specialises in a particular skill.

So, LinkedIn is a very powerful means to expand your professional network without having to really do the legwork of physically going out and meeting people up and down the country. It enables you to ask question to the people you need to rub shoulders with and develop your network.

You will find a group within the LinkedIn website called Jobs In F1 that you can subscribe to and you can follow updates from other members in the group. Updates are posted into the LinkedIn group by the Jobs in F1 team, and also by the recruiters and other people either working or interested in the F1 industry.

LinkedIn is a good forum for discussion about any technical ideas that you may have, and it is monitored by the Jobs in F1 team so that we can see which kind of job you are interested in and we can look at pairing you with the right F1 opportunities. We can also use it as a means to contact you and let you know when suitable opportunities are advertised.

Don't forget to go to jobs posting and find the team pages. You can do the legwork yourself by typing the team name followed by F1 or the word racing, and if jobs are available they will be listed. Make a note of the name of the company at the bottom of the page that has listed the jobs, click the save the job button, and then click the view button, the name of the person that posted the job is shown in the top right hand corner of the screen. Write down that name of the advertising company or save it to your data base file, pick up the telephone and speak to them. Don't forget to search on the Internet for the recruiter that posted the jobs, they may have more jobs that have not yet been put online.

It can be hard to find F1 companies on LinkedIn; sometimes the team name is not mentioned in the URL. Jobs In F1 has already done this and you can view the list in the member's area at **www.jobsinf1.com.** We have also added a number of other connections to help you build your network. The list is published online because like most organisations you get a turnover of staff and we need to keep it relevant.

To build your network LinkedIn has a great feature called "People At" – then the company name is shown. You get names, pictures, job descriptions and when you click on the individual featured it takes you to their LinkedIn profile page and also shows you their contacts as well, this will help you build your F1 connections. To navigate your way around LinkedIn rules scroll to the bottom of the page and see which groups that member belongs too. Apply to join the group and if accepted you can then make direct contact to join that persons network.

When you look at someone's profile it shows you how you are connected to that individual on the side of the page. You can ask your existing connections to introduce you, especially if you have a contact name that you would like to reach.

One final but possibly direct method if you have had no success by applying through the advised routes is to use your list of individual names and utilise the companies Internet presence.

Many companies have a simple email address system, you could chance you arm and drop an email directly to an engineer or team member that is currently performing the job you would like to do and asking if they could offer you some mentoring. Make sure you include your links to your LinkedIn profile, your website or video interview and don't forget to send your CV and a cover letter describing the job you are interested in. If it is related to a specific job application make sure you use the job description and reference number, you could ask if the role advertised complements your ability. Your CV may be passed to HR with some encouraging words.

YOUTUBE

Not many people really recognise the value of having a video interview. People are quite often surprised to find out that YouTube is actually a search engine being used by recruiters. We get on the Internet every day, and look for all kinds of items, and YouTube is a very powerful tool. By creating a video interview for YouTube, you can control the content, you can guide the interview and the person that is recruiting into understanding what you would like to tell them about yourself, you have time to relax, edit and amend a video as required so that you can quite simply present yourself in the most professional manner.

You could also use, for example, a PowerPoint presentation and project it onto the wall behind you where you could even describe some of your ideas or theories that would benefit an F1 team. You have to recognise that the world with the internet is a very different place to how things used to be done, and people still very much follow the traditional routes for their recruitment policies as far as contacting agencies or advertising in the press, and use all those standard means in order to advertise a job.

The Internet allows you to turn that on its head and to present yourself in a new way. The whole point of this is what makes you stand out from other applicants. How easy and novel would it be to put your tablet device down on the table and ask the interviewer to watch your 1-2 minute (maximum) video presentation, think about how much information you could provide to the interviewer.

Go to www.youtube.com and sign up. It's really easy to upload your video, just click on the button at the top of the screen, select your file and click upload.

VIDEO INTERVIEW

Most of us have a smartphone, and the quality of video that can be taken on a smartphone today is very good. In addition to that, what you require is a reasonable quality microphone, it is important that the recruiter is able to hear clearly what you're saying without background noise and echoing.

- A good quality microphone offers high quality sound and a lapel microphone with a about a 6m cable will be discrete in your video. The background noise and echo is reduced with this type of microphone so you get great audio.
- To work in conjunction with your microphone you need an adapter cable that plugs into your smart phone jack.
- A Tripod is an essential piece of kit because nobody likes to watch a shaking camera video.
- Tripod adapter is needed to hold your smart phone or high definition video camera

- Shadows do not look good on a video; you are not making a horror movie, make sure you look good by using a light deflector umbrella.
- Most computers can be used to edit your video, on a MacBook using iMovie, alternatively on a Windows PC using Moviemaker.

Visit the member's area at **www.jobsinf1.com** to see our recommended video equipment.

CREATE YOUR OWN WEBSITE

What does creating a website have to do with getting a job?

We all get on the Internet or some social tool everyday, one of the biggest portals is Google. By creating your own webpage, you can choose the content that you would like to put online to represent yourself professionally, and you are not limited by guidelines or the restrictions of using other websites like a job search site or LinkedIn as far as the profile information that they would like you to make public.

This is an opportunity for you to put added value contents about your job, your career and your interests and your CV. You could, for example, sit on the wheel of your racing car and just give a basic description of your car, your interests, any modifications that you may have made to your vehicle, and take this as an opportunity for you to demonstrate your skills through the use of a video.

What you have to remember is that your webpage is your shop window to the world, and this is how you sell yourself. It is a great means to self promote your skills and ability by adding your digital CV to your website. You can also add your social media accounts for LinkedIn, Facebook and Twitter to your webpage.

In the modern world potential employers view people's social profiles, posts and their online presence. You should consider creating professional profiles for social media sites like Twitter and Facebook. You may not wish a potential employer to read your friends social post that may cause you embarrassment.

Jobs In F1 has created professional sites for Facebook, Twitter and LinkedIn so that you can use them as your professional community.

You can use your webpage to describe how passionate you are about F1. It's a good opportunity for you to demonstrate your knowledge of the sport, as well as obviously listing your academic and professional achievements. And throughout the book we talk about strategies to get yourself noticed and what sets you apart from any other candidate.

It would also be very simple for you to put an electronic tablet on the table to show an interviewer a visually impressive video CV.

It is now easier than ever to create a webpage, you simply need to go online and to buy a domain name and a hosting package, download a page theme and you will have access to start to build a webpage. A good tool for doing this is called WordPress, this is a very simple tool to use and with a little bit of trial and error, you can simply choose a layout theme, add text, add pictures, add videos and put your website online.

There is no need to spend hundreds of pounds paying someone to create a website, Jobs In F1 offers courses in website creation and you will be able to set up and create your webpage with very little expense or effort. We will also describe simply how to optimise your website so that you can be headhunted rather than spend hours searching for your F1 Job.

12. GETTING HEADHUNTED

Ordinarily to be headhunted, you need to have a personal contact with somebody, and that person would be endorsing your skills and your abilities to perform the job that is required. This is still an effective tool today, and this is why Jobs in F1 has put together a strategy that enables you to establish those personal contacts by using social media tools, by using Facebook, Twitter and LinkedIn, and by using the traditional job searching sites or recruitment agencies.

If you do not have that personal contact, then you will have a reliance on search engines and the optimisation of your CV in order for those companies to find you. And what you have to appreciate is that a search engine is a tool, and it's used to search for specific words and phrases, and has been programmed to search for a specific written criteria. So, in order for your CV to be found by that search engine, you have to fulfil that exact written criteria.

Jobs in F1 has put together a comprehensive list of all the job titles and descriptions used by the F1 teams when they are seeking a vacancy to be fulfilled. So, let's say for example, that an F1 team is looking for a CFD senior designer, you will need to have that exact phrase matched on your CV in order for them to find you.

Alternatively, you may need to be seeking the position of Senior Aerodynamic Designer; this is actually the same job as CFD senior designer. By putting right phrase into your search criteria and saving that on an agents website in the email notifications, you will receive an email every time a job with that description is uploaded onto an online job site. This does not necessarily mean, however, that you will only receive that email about F1 jobs; you will receive a general email about any job of that description, but they are likely to in an industry that may give you valued experience that is transferrable to F1.

What you have to do is use other key words, for example the name of a particular F1 team that you may be interested in. You may also want to add the words F1 or even just the description F1 to your search criteria. So, by putting this collective group of keywords together, you're optimising your opportunity for either a search engine to notify you, or for a headhunter to find your CV.

Arranging the Interview

You will usually be contacted by telephone if an agency, contracting house or HR personnel believes you may be a viable candidate, you will also receive an email. The interviewer will usually have set a single day aside to conduct a series of interviews, so agreeing to the date offered is your best option.

The agency or contacting house will want to ask a few questions about your background, experience and aspirations. You may be asked if you intend to seek a contract or employed position

If you have been headhunted it is easy to be over enthusiastic in agreeing what is being offered. Discussing pay used to be a reserve of the interview but today it is becoming more common for recruiters to find out what you are prepared to work for before the interview. Sending candidates that cannot agree terms does not reflect well on the recruiter.

Rather than give the recruiter a salary or contracting rate expectation you should provide a range, this leave room for negotiation at the interview. Sometimes what is explained on the job description does not represent everything that may be required from you. I have never read a job description that stated you may need to work 15 hours a day when the going gets tough.

What you should do is ask the agent what package is on offer and if they think there is any flexibility in the offer.

13. THE INTERVIEW

PUNCTUALITY & PREPARATION

It is essential that when you arrive for your interview that you are punctual, the person that arrives late or is sweating and flustered when they arrive because they have run from car park or station is not going to be in the right frame of mind and will start the interview at a disadvantage. If you are late the interviewer will not be very impressed with you. It is a particular character trait of everyone at an F1 company that everything must be predictable and you have to meet your deadline. A car with three tyres at a pit stop is no good to anyone; the opportunity has passed.

It is highly likely that they plan to see several candidates in one day, if you are late they may consider that there is not enough time to perform your interview.

You should aim to be in the facility at least 30 minutes before the interview, you might have to get through gatehouse security, and find a parking space in a busy car park. Aim to be in the building 20 minutes before the interview, you may have to walk a short distance to the reception. In some F1 company buildings there are multiple receptions. You need to be able to pace steadily through the building, use this time relax and put yourself in the right frame of mind. Some of the buildings are stunning with F1 cars on display, they are impressive but don't be overwhelmed, remember why you are there.

I like to take in the surroundings feel comfortable with them. I think about a script for the interview a few days before, it is a two-way conversation and while they have specific questions they need to ask, you should have specific information you would like to discuss.

F1 MENTALITY

If you need any help getting into the right mind-set we have a few tips that may assist you in your interview conversation. The most important lesson I learnt is to be able to characterise a components material and functional properties, or those of a system, and to be able to predict how it would perform in different environments and under different load conditions, analysing the potential failures and designing them out. Always be compulsively comprehensive in your preparation.

A package of small changes can make a big advantage. You've got to consider everything that may affect the car, the aerodynamics, the tyres, the weather, the humidity, the temperature; it all has a major impact. You constantly have to evaluate your ideas and your own performance.

There are rules and guidelines, I can choose to interpret those any way I see fit that will gain me an advantage over the competitors and within the spirit of the regulations.

I take my competitors seriously, I look at what they do, analyse it, and then I look to do it better.

I never consider that there are problems, only a series of challenges to overcome.

What kind of technology can I use and get exclusive access to so that no other team can copy it. e.g. a specialised brake disc compound, or a new higher strength lighter weight carbon ply.

You've got to know what you're going to do before you do it. Sometime you only get one chance to get something right. If you don't work as a team, it all goes wrong. You have to be prepared for something to go wrong. You've got to keep a clear head, never panic because there is a job to be done.

If there is a job to be done, then I'm going to do it. I am prepared to work smart and hard, and not leave till the job is done. Many engineers and mechanics put in a lot of hours, during peaks to get new parts designed, prototyped, tested and on a car for the imminent race, the working day can be from 6:00am to 21:00pm. Why do you do it? Because you love what you do and you are a part of a team, and you all take care of each other.

Finally a few quotes:

- Second place is just the first of the losers.
- Winning is the only thing that matters.

- You have to have a single-minded determination and be able to work within a team.
- Nobody wants to be associated with a loser, work harder and think smarter than the competition and become a winner.
- Look to gain every single advantage, no matter how small.
- It helps to believe that you are better at your job than anybody else as long as you can step up and meet your own and their expectations.
- Above all be prepared.

APPEARANCE & GREETING

It is important that you look smart and you look professional. All the details are critical, a full suit, neatly pressed, clean shirt, nice tie, polished shoes, smart looking watch, because we've all heard the expression, 'You can tell a lot about a person by their shoes and their watch.' You need to look the part, you need to look sharper, you need to look smarter than the next person coming in for an interview, because you're competing with the best of the best, and you need to have an F1 mentality where every small detail, every small advantage that you can gain is a difference between a winner and a loser.

Whilst you are waiting for your interviewer in the reception area, stay on your feet, nobody looks good sat down, lounging around in a big sofa chair, with a suit on, and if you sit there with your shirt pulling out of your trousers and with your jacket spilled wide open, you may not create the right first impression. If you stay on your feet, your suit looks clean, it looks straight, it looks sharp and you're already in a position to welcome the interviewer, to step forward and shake their hand as they approach you. This helps to break down any barriers, and it gives the impression that you're ready for action.

A firm, but not over tight handshake grip should be used. The grip indicates strength of character, a dominance of mind and control. When putting your hand forward your hand and fingers should be straight and with fingers pointing downwards and thumb to the sky. You should also welcome them with a smile, and be sure to

use their name when welcoming them, let them know it's a pleasure to meet them. Let them lead the way to the interview room, follow close behind and be sure to initiate the conversation and engage in an interest of their workload and what they are working on. If you initiate the conversation, it puts the interviewer at ease. They may just impart a little information that you can reference during the interview, but only if you had covered that topic in your preparations.

THE INTERVIEW

An interview works both ways, the team are looking to assess if you have the capabilities to perform the role, and you have to be sure that the job and offer being made is in your interest to accept.

During the interview, sit upright, don't slouch; you should lean forwards slightly, as though you're engaged in the conversation, because you are. Listen carefully to what they say and answer the question concisely, don't waffle.

Be sure to be familiar with your CV, a lot of people use the technique of just running through your CV and asking specific questions about points on it. Other interviewers will have a format that they wish to follow.

When the interviewer speaks, be sure to engage in eye contact for the first few seconds of listening to them, it lets them know that you're paying attention.

During your interview, you will need to open up to the interviewer, to show them your personality, what inspires you and what is your interest, this is a key point in the interview process, because this is your opportunity to leave them with a thought or a memory that will leave a lasting impression. I would advise using something that is relevant to the subject matter. For example, when I was six years of age, I was introduced to a gentleman called Colin Chapman, the founder of Lotus Cars, and this came about because my father had a job working on the first version of the Lotus Esprit. I described for the interviewer how the opportunity made me feel to be sat in the first ever Lotus Esprit and how my father built the car and underwater hull for the car that was used in the James Bond film The Spy Who Loved

Me, and how Colin Chapman joked that I was a future engineer when I kept asking about the car and how it worked.

There is always the part of the interview when contract and money need to be discussed. The HR department and interviewer will already have an idea of how they value the job, this would have been provided to the agent at the time of advertisement or HR will raise the topic, and they will look to secure the lowest offer, its business.

So not to cause any offense the best thing that you can say to negotiate a better deal is "it's a little lower than what I am used to earning", and then say nothing until the interviewer speaks. If a salary or contract rate has already been presented the interviewer may offer something more.

It is likely that you may have to relocate to support your F1 career and some teams are located in places that demand a higher cost of living. Make sure you have fully researched the cost of living in the local area.

During your interview be sure not to use any slang, rude or potentially offensive language, do not complain or whinge about any previous assignments, contracts or bosses. This will not be looked upon with any favour.

QUESTIONS YOU MAY BE ASKED

- Would you like a tea or coffee? This is a good way for the interviewer to see if a candidate is relaxed or if their hand shakes under pressure. Accept a cup of water but do not drink it. When a candidate needs thinking time they reach for the cup to take a drink in an attempt to buy a few seconds. An experienced interviewer will see this and be listening for a shaking cup & saucer. They are looking for a person that remains confident and calm under pressure.

- What were your responsibilities at this company (on your CV)? Start with your most recent activities and key achievement.

- What inspired your interest in applying for the role? A Passion for the sport. Being given the opportunity to fulfil a life-long ambition and to demonstrate my capability as part of a team. The opportunity to learn or similar responses should be from the heart.

- Please look at this picture of a 3D object and tell me which of the 2D images fold into the shape.
- What is the answer to this mathematical question?
- How is this part manufactured?
- Would you apply any special process to manufacture it?
- Do you see any driving characteristics of our car or drivers?
- What impact would that have to the car?
- Please remember these setting details, we will ask you to confirm the settings in a few minutes.
- How did you choose your dissertation topic?
- What problems did you need to overcome?
- How did you research the solution to the problem?
- Can you remember the settings we showed you?
- What do you know of the next year regulations?
- How would you meet this requirement?
- What have you done that shows a commitment to go above and beyond any task assigned to you?
- Tell me about you personal life?
- Do you take part in any motorsport activity?
- Are you affiliated to any organisations?
- What makes you better than any other candidate that I have spoken to today?
- Are you happy with the remuneration offered?
- Do you have any questions?

You should always have questions, is this company right for you?

- What is the next stage of the appointment process?
- Is the role what you were expecting? Have they explained everything to you?
- Ask to see the working environment or facilities.
- Ask what tools they use to design the car, or what equipment they have in the manufacturing department.
- Ask to see the trophy cabinet. The history of the team is written in gold and silver.

WHAT IS EXPECTED IN A CANDIDATE

I sincerely believe that you will be able to make informative decisions and understand what you will be expected to achieve as you study and plan your career whether that be as an engineer or any other role you chose to pursue for a career in F1.

Academic achievement is not always enough, attitude and character also need to be developed and you will not find advice on this in an engineering text book, so expand your personal development, study biographies and personal development books.

Successful people have the following underlying character traits:

- Leadership and an acceptance of responsibility,
- An ambition and a plan of what they would like to achieve,
- A strong belief in their capability to achieve,
- They are self-motivating and will not rely on others to do things for them; and be able to listen and work as part of a team,
- Nothing beats preparation, they pay attention to detail and consider all factors and scenarios and make educated predictions and self fulfilling prophecies,

- Endurance and a tenacity to see a task through to completion,

Other traits expected in a candidate are:

- An in depth knowledge of your discipline, and profession,
- To show respect for your colleagues and a politeness to listen,
- To be personable and open to approach and be prepared to spend your time investing in building a relationship with your colleagues and suppliers, people are prepared to go the extra mile for a friend,
- An ability to understand and focus on your role,
- An attitude to work till the job is done,
- A pride to work for yourself and for your team,

Personality is part hereditary and part conditioning of your environment, so condition your mind to succeed, be yourself and focus on your plan. We are all unique, so why be ordinary.

14. WHAT IS THE POINT OF FORMULA 1?

I was once asked, what is the point of Formula 1?

- So lets not be coy about the primary answer, F1 exists to make money, and lots of it. The better the team performs the more money it makes in sponsorship and merchandising, it is a business.
- To win, collect trophies and prove you are better than anyone else in the world.
- F1 is a global entertainment business. People are attracted to the excitement of open wheel racing, to see a driver pass another competitor and seeing man and machine and physical limits working in synergy, and the glory of victory. Although nobody would wish any harm to the driver or any member of the team an unexpected incident puts people on the edge of their seat and adds to the excitement.
- For those involved in the sport it is an extremely rewarding and fun way to earn a living and travel the world, and for the drivers the spoils of glory.
- People have a fascination with learning about new technologies, and F1 generates technology and innovation in abundance, and showcases it like no other medium. Its contribution to engineering design and design tools, material development and innovative manufacturing processes is rarely matched. Patents are created and technologies are fed into the mainstream automotive market that you enjoy on a daily basis.
- F1 encourages people into the career of engineering, and surprisingly there is a shortage of engineers foreseen within the next decade. Engineering is an amazingly rewarding career; it draws out everything that is great in a person from creative thinking, to teamwork, pride in yourself and your colleagues, and the satisfaction of contributing to the advancement of humankind.
- Racing is also a great way for OEM car manufacturers to try out technical ideas in extreme conditions and they can be tested and

proven without some of the heavy regulation and governance of the automotive industry.

- The glamour, and the scale of events like Monaco draw the wealthy and powerful and this is an opportunity to showcase their wealth and opulence.
- We all enjoy the comradeship of fellow supporters.

15. JOBS IN F1

Just like any other company that produces a product you have the standard business infrastructure and roles to be performed. Each team varies in size but teams will employ anywhere between 200 and 1000 employees and contractors. This may seem a little obvious to experienced personnel but this book will be read by all ages. As a child at school I had no idea of what a company structure was or what roles people did in an F1 company.

Depending on each team there are subtle differences in the extent of responsibility and many of the roles interact together or are multi-disciplined, so to explain them we have put them into the following categories:

- Company Structure & Organisation Roles
- Vehicle Systems & Design Roles
- Race Team

COMPANY STRUCTURE & OPERATIONS

EXECUTIVES

Owners

Traditionally race drivers or designers, but in today's world corporate brands and vehicle manufacturers own some of the teams.

Directors

Directors are a board of senior officials that manage all activities across the business and make the key decisions on the company's technical and commercial direction.

- Managing Director
- Technical Director
- Sporting Director
- Operations Director

- Commercial & Financial Director
- Director of Design & Development Programmes
- Manufacturing Director
- Facility Director
- Team Principle

FINANCE

Manage the company's financial funds, set budgets for managing the company and the development of the cars.

- **Chief Financial Officer** – Manages the finances of the company, manages affairs with the bank, lawyers and auditors to ensure obligations are met.
- **Head of Finance** - Ensures bills are paid on time, PAYE, Payroll, manages cash-flow, sets credit control, bank reconciliation, invoices, production of balance sheets.
- **Accountant** – Takes care of the company's accounts and tax affairs, VAT and corporation tax and auditors.
- **Account Managers** – Deal with sponsors and supplier accounts to ensure multi-currency income revenue is received and managed to agreement.

HUMAN RESOURCE

Deal with all matters relating to staff employment, working conditions and benefits and health and safety for the whole company.

- **Head of HR** – Is responsible for recruitment, attending interviews and issuing contracts for employees and contractors. Keeps up to date with the latest employment laws and manages staff issues.
- **HR Assistants** – Deal with reviewing CV's, booking interviews and HR admin. Advertises jobs and sets up interviews, and deals with agents.

INFRASTRUCTURE & IT

Ensure the smooth operation of the company.

- **Head of Infrastructure** – Performs a few roles, they ensure that everyone in the team can be contacted at anytime and that communication links are established between the headquarters and the race team. That all data can be transferred correctly within the team. Manages the IT infrastructure and operating systems at the headquarters.
- **IT Engineer** – Develops the information systems and application at headquarters to allow the sharing of information and assist in the developing the companies electronic processes.
- **IT Infrastructure Technician** - IT Helpdesk service support.
- **IT Infrastructure Technician** (Race Team) - will organise and deploy support for the IT systems at race and track test events.
- **Mathematician** – Will develop the complex algorithms required to support vehicle development and race strategies.
- **AX Dynamics Analyst/Developer** - creates specific operational business processes and core resource planning (ERP) for material control, finance and HR management.

LEGAL

A degree in law & business and knowledge of engineering is essential.

- **Lawyer** – Will protect the companies brand, copyright and commercial business affairs like intellectual property, sponsorship deals, and protect them from issues with motorsports governance or media stories.

MARKETING

Good communication and people skills are essential. A degree in any of the following is preferred but not essential - marketing, business, English, history, PR, media studies, journalism or communications.

- **Head of Communication** - Approves information releases to the media and the world press.

- **Sponsorship Manager** – Is responsible to acquire and retain world-class sponsors and raise funds by selling advertising space on the cars and merchandise.
- **Marketing Research Analyst** – Provides input to the commercial and sponsorship manager by researching companies thought to be sponsorship candidates and writing personnel biographies of people in the business.
- **Head of Hospitality** – will ensure that the team and esteemed guests are well cared for and also that their day at the Grand Prix is as comfortable as possible. Also manages the hospitality staff and organises the daily events in the hospitality suite.
- **Hospitality Staff** x 5-10 people entertain guests, wait tables and serve food and drinks and keep the hospitality suite clean at the Grand Prix.
- **Head of Merchandising** – promotes the team products to increase income revenue through the sale of shirts, hats & flags etc.
- **Press Officer** – Is a point of contact for the media and investors. Attends Grand Prix and sets up press conferences and interviews to promote the team. They manage the website content and liaise with journalists & VIP's and check that any information passed to the newspapers, TV, and radio represents the company professionally whether visual, written or oral.
- **Digital Communications Manager** - Manages press release distribution systems on social media channels and website content.

ADMINISTRATION PLANNING & CONTROL

- **Head of Planning & Control** – Oversees all project management activities.
- **Project Managers** – Plan and organise the development activities of the cars systems and components and work with all departments across the business to ensure everything is done on time, within budget and to the right quality.

- **BOM Administrators** – (Bill of Materials) Keep a track of changes requested by engineering for design updates to the vehicle. Keep purchasing informed of what needs to be bought and manufacturing what to build.
- **PA's** (Personal Assistants) work for the executive team and will take care of their administration and organisational tasks.
- **Receptionists** – Will answer the phone and carry out administration tasks.
- **Travel Co-ordinator** – Arranges all of the companies travel, book flights, hotels, restaurants, organises medical certificates and entrance visas. Given that between 60-100 people travel to a Grand Prix this is no small task.

PROCUREMENT

Place the purchase orders to buy everything the company needs.

- **Head of Purchasing** – will oversee all contracts and purchasing activities, agrees final cost for the BOM.
- **Purchasing** – Source suppliers and negotiate costs for commodities and components.
- **Buyers** – Place orders for materials based on stock levels or new orders.
- **Supply Chain Manager** – Ensures the entire supply chain from raw materials and processing to manufacture, assembly and delivery produce the highest quality product from the outset.

MATERIAL CONTROL

Control the stock of parts and materials.

- **Material Controllers** - ensure that there are sufficient stock supplies of materials and components used to build the cars and support development and testing are available on a daily basis. Requirements are passed to the buyers or ordered by an MRP system.
- **Supplier Quality** – Ensure that the supplier has all of the information they need to make the parts and that they are manufactured

exactly as the design team intended. They ensure the supplier has a quality system like ISO9000 or TS16949 accreditation and can produce quality parts.

- **Goods Inspectors** – Check and measure parts that arrive at the factory to ensure they are to the correct design ordered by the purchasing team and that all significant or critical part characteristics have been met.
- **Stores** – Organise parts and materials and deliver them to the production area when needed by the mechanics to build the cars.
- **Quality Engineers** – Will make sure that the car has been built to process, using the correct parts, to an acceptable standard both mechanically and visually.
- **Process Engineer** – Develops special manufacturing processes for new technologies and ensures parts are built to a repeatable process to ensure quality of car manufacture.

FACILITY

Everything related to the building fixtures and fittings, the health of the building and gardens.

- **Factory Manager** – Makes sure everyone has a safe environment to work in, and that all technical systems in the building operate like lights, heating and air conditioning keep people healthy and happy in the work place.
- **Maintenance Team** – Are engineers that look after the building, service equipment and gardens.
- **Cleaners** – Protect the health and safety of all employees and guests.

CATERING

Fuelling the team with food and drink.

- **Chef** x2 (Race Team) - Set the menu for a nutritional team diet and localised menu for the guests at each Grand Prix, prepare the food.

- **Kitchen Assistance** x2 (Race Team) - Prepare the food.
- **Catering team** - Headquarters may have to feed from to 200 to 1000 people on a daily basis.

MANUFACTURING & PRODUCTION

Manufacture parts, assemble components, build sub-systems and race cars.

- **Head of Production** – Has overall responsibility for the manufacturing facility and equipment, health and safety, the manufacturing of parts, and assembly of the cars. Responsible for recruiting production staff. Ensures the build facility is kept meticulously clean like a laboratory.
- **Production Coordinator** – Ensures everyone in the factory knows what needs to be done and by when, that they have the tools, equipment and parts required to do the job.
- **Technical Operations Manager** – Train & mentor personnel to develop technical solutions for production manufacturing, process and equipment.
- **Manufacturing Engineer** – Designs manufacturing processes, jigs and fixtures used to assemble sub-systems and the car and ensures repeatability of quality in production.
- **Composites**
    - **Head of Composites** – Manages the composite department.
    - **Composite Lead Design Engineer** – Oversees composite development with a strong knowledge of structural engineering applications, composite materials selection, surface treatment and test specifications.
    - **Composite Process Engineer** – Develops new techniques and documents repeatable processes to ensure quality.
    - **Composite Manufacturing**
        - **Laminating Supervisor** - Organises workloads and monitors the preparation and lay up of the carbon fibre

sheet panels before autoclave oven baking, ensures quality and accuracy of all completed jobs.

- **Composite Laminators Technician** - will layout the complex carbon composite laminations sheets for manufacturing into components. It is critical the right structure of carbon ply is used and the orientation of the material correct to support the design, stress and strength requirements.
- **Autoclave operator** – Manages the oven used to cure the carbon fibre, each part has a unique curing cycle. Ensures the lay up has been bagged correctly to ensure the vacuum squeeze compresses the layers together, and manages the high temperatures to ensure resin infusion to the carbon fibre.
- **Bodyshell Fabricator** – Machines or trims and fits the panels to vehicle. Prepares the body panels with additional fixing for assembly to the car by the mechanics.

o **Composite Quality Inspector** – Conducts geometrical and process inspection to ensure the quality of the parts.

PAINT TEAM

Paint technicians - Create the stunning paint finish to the bodywork. They need to prepare the composite panels so that the paint will adhere and ensure a dust & silicone free environment to ensure that the paint does not lift. They mix the paints and paint the panels. Like any part on an F1 car paint is weight that needs to be minimised so the technique used by the technician is critical to ensure full coverage with minimum weight. The air brushing technique is used to create the fine detailed finishing that blends one colour into another.

MACHINING & MODEL SHOP

- **Machinist** – Operates a flatbed lathe machine to make parts or tools. Experience on Hardinge or Hitachi Seiki lathes, Mazak & Mikron CNC Machines is favourable.

- **Machinist Turner** - Operates a turning lathe to manufacture highly accurate turned components, CNC lathe experience is preferred.
- **CAM Programmers** (Computer Aided Model) (CATIA V5) - Extract information from CAD system and write machining programmes.
- **Laser Cutter Operator** – Computer Aided cutting of sheet metal or other materials for folding or pressing in to finished parts.
- **Pattern Shop CNC Machine Tool Programmer** (Computer Numerically Controlled Machine) - Sets programming and cutters on three and five axis machines for each material and part to produce models or tooling. Operates the CNC machine.
- **Model Maker** – Produce 3D models from drawing by hand or with CAD models for 3D printing or stereolithography processes for the wind tunnel testing and to assist the patternmakers
- **Pattern Makers** – Produce 3D tool patterns used to make the tooling that is used for manufacturing parts including moulds for carbon fibre lay up and metal or composite castings, pressing or resin infusion.

BUILD TEAM

- **No2 Mechanic** - Has the primary responsibility to build the car in the factory before it is shipped to test or race. Works with and oversees the sub-assembly mechanics and raises build issue with the design office. Assembles cars for rig testing and works on mock-ups of the car and assemblies.
- **Mechanics** – Build the car and check each other's work to ensure quality and correct torques and process are used to minimise failures.
- **Sub-assembly Mechanic** – Pre-assembles systems before installation to the car.

- **Fabricator** – will make bespoke components or modify parts for the cars if required.
- **Race Team Bodywork & Sticker Technician** will work closely with the graphic designer.

GRAPHIC DESIGN

Graphic Designers – Create the artwork for the sponsor's logo on the car, and images for the company promotional pictures.

Helmet design is now becoming a popular fashion in F1. Drivers may have new designs for each race or special team event.

QUALITY

- **Quality Manager** – Will oversee quality of the parts being built both externally and internally for the vehicle systems. Rejects parts that do not meet the requirements of the design and quality departments. Oversees a team of measurement and inspection specialists that use visual, physical measurement, ultrasonic and x-ray techniques to prove components are fit for purpose.

- **Quality Assurance Manager** - Develops internal company processes and instructions to ensure human error is minimalised.

- **Supplier Quality Assurance Engineer** – Deal with all supplier issues, audit the supplier capabilities and verify that supplier manufacturing processes and materials will deliver the results required by manufacturing and the race team. Ensure that the supplier has all of the information they need to make the parts, and that they are manufactured exactly as the design team intended. They ensure the supplier has a quality system like ISO9000 or TS16949 accreditation and can consistently produce quality parts.

- **Goods Inspectors** – Check and measure parts that arrive at the factory to ensure they are to the correct design ordered by the purchasing team, and that all significant or critical part characteristics have been met.

- **Stores** – Organise parts and materials, pick kits and delivers them to the production area when needed by the mechanics to build the cars.

- **Quality Engineering** – Will make sure that the car has been built to acceptable standard mechanically, visually and within the FIA requirements.

- **Process Engineer** – Develops special manufacturing processes for new technologies and ensures parts are built to a repeatable process to ensure quality of car manufacture

LOGISTICS

- **Logistic Manager** – Oversees all Logistics, ensures the health and safety of the logistic team and that all equipment is supplied to minimise injury. Plans the logistic calendar and oversees all actions are in place to load trucks with the required equipment to support the race team and that all items are correctly identified and administered so not to cause any delay at international customs. Confirms travel requirements to the travel co-ordinator. Supports the race team with any last minute requests for parts to be sent to the track.

- Race Team Logistics

    - **Truck Transporter Driver** (Race Team) delivers the cars, garage equipment and hospitality units to the race and test tracks.

    - **Truckie** – Loads & Un-loads the trucks and sets up the teams hospitality unit and garage at the GP.

- **Logistics Assistant** – Manages the checklists to ensure every item required on the trucks has been accounted for and is loaded correctly to avoid damage during transport.

STORES

- **Stores Manager** – Checks every part in and out of the factory and keeps track of stock levels and shortages in the ERP system. Quarantines parts that need further inspection.

- **Stores Operative** – Assists in the unloading of trucks and drives the fork lift. Places parts in the correct stores location. Maintains cleanliness in the stores and goods in area.

- **Kitters** – Pick all parts for a complete system that requires assembly and takes them to the build area.

VEHICLE SYSTEMS & DESIGN ROLES

The Design Process

All personnel contribute to understanding the FIA regulations each department head contributes to cross-functional team discussion to deliver the design concept.

Project management runs the programme to agreed milestones, including technical delivery, cost and weight control. There is close interaction with manufacturing, CAD engineers, CAE Engineers, FEA engineers, procurement, supplier sourcing and management, VA VE cost and process engineering, problem & risk resolution, BOM control and change management via a drawing release system, APQP quality process deployment, PFMEA, DFMEA and DVP.

In many of the design disciplines knowledge of CAN communication and calibration protocols are standard practice and used by all electronic units to communicate and share data that is then transmitted to the pit wall.

All engineers regardless of discipline aim to maximise performance & strength and reliability whilst minimising size, weight and cost.

When designing a component or system an engineer needs to truly understand every aspect of the entire lifecycle of the components. To do this you need to define the purpose and the functional requirement of the components, and put together a specification that takes into consideration how and where this part will be used on the car as well as how the part will be subjected to punishment by its surrounding environment. You need to determine the material properties that suit the functional targets and the working environment, and then assess how the materials and mechanical properties may change under the working conditions and the potential for that part to fail. Then you engineer out the potential for failure.

A great deal is known about existing material properties & composition and this is used to calculate characteristics like, material modulus, stress, strain, stiffness / youngs modulus, shear strength, toughness, hardness, density & mass, thermal coefficient, electrical conductivity and resistance, effects of vibration, temperature and humidity.

You also need to have a good idea of how to manufacture the parts and any specific process required to manipulate the chosen materials to the required design that maintains the material properties required.

For electronic and electrical parts you need to have defined the schematics, chosen components and have developed a software strategy that covers the functional and failure strategies to a safe conclusion.

Once this is done you can commence the CAD (computer aided design) work, the whole car is designed in 3D and the kinematic movements checked. CAD designers make a major contribution to the layout and package of the cars design, so it comes as a surprise to many that CAD designers may not have a degree. Experience, skill and commitment are required and a degree certainly helps a CAD designer. Their knowledge and ingenuity to overcome design issues is exceptional and they work hand in hand with the responsible engineer that approves the design.

Most of the systems on an F1 car require CFD (computational fluid dynamics), basically every part that you can see on the car, and a few you cannot like the F-Duct, cooling and hydraulics. Aerodynamic CFD models the virtual airflow over the car, and to do this a mathematical mesh is created on the surface of the car. As the parameters of the test like airflow, velocity, humidity, altitude and lateral G's are introduced the mesh moves under the theoretical forces applied and you can begin to predict how the air will travel over the car, as the downforces are created the amount of drag can be witnessed.

Wind tunnel models will be created to physically prove out the aerodynamic design. This is then correlated to the simulations run, the simulation model is then updated to improve the predictions of the cars performance.

Once the parts have been designed a team of suppliers and in house experts manufacture the components, these are built into components or sub-systems for assembly to the car. Every part of the car will be tested beyond the limit of its design target. This is to ensure reliability of the design.

One of the major sets of testing to be carried out is crash testing the monocoque chassis, nose cone and rear impact structure. Fourteen crash scenarios are conducted and the FIA attend all of the tests to homologate the chassis for race use.

For technical details of an F1 car design and assembly visit **www.jobsinf1.com** and view our technical pages.

The design team roles are explained in further detail in the following section.

THE JOBS IN F1 DESIGN

Each team uses slightly different titles for a number of similar jobs, and in some cases the extent of responsibility varies a little from team to team, an experienced engineer will see areas where these overlaps may exist, but the following job descriptions explain the principle role and a number of disciplines that may be shared in a team. External suppliers will also design and develop some of the cars sub-systems.

In the following job descriptions we are not explaining the detailed technical design of the car, but are explaining the key vehicle systems, the engineering roles, and the tools used by the engineers and designers. This will help you to decide your vocational discipline and help you to choose your educational courses.

Please note that heads of departments participate in a number of meetings to specifically discuss the development progress and results with the chief designer, meet with suppliers and have a department to manage, resource to assign and budgets and timing to be kept.

AERODYNAMIC ENGINEERS

An F1 Aerodynamicist requires a background in mathematics and physics with skills in Matlab and ideally a modern OO language such as Java/C#.

The role of an aerodynamicist is to maximise the cars performance by shaping the bodywork to create the most downforce with the least drag.

- **Chief Aerodynamicist** - Responsible for whole vehicle aerodynamics, interprets the regulations and defines the aerodynamic principles for the car design, disseminates the requirement to the team.
- **Head of Computational Fluid Dynamics (CFD)** - Oversees all computational simulation.
- **Senior CFD Aerodynamicist (Team Leader)** - Responsible for the shaping of the bodywork and key systems and parts of the car, and studies the overall performance of the whole car aerodynamics.
- **CFD Aerodynamicist** - Aerodynamicists work on the computational fluid dynamics (CFD) and surface of an individual piece of the body design, or the whole car to study the effects of every small change. This is to develop the body shape and wings design using a virtual wind tunnel on a computer screen. This precedes the manufacturing of the expensive wind tunnel models that provide further evidence of the aerodynamic capability.
- **CFD Aerodynamicist / Thermodynamicist** - Develops the cooling systems on the vehicle with CFD analysis of airflow through the vehicle, radiators and cooling fluid flow through the powertrain.
- **Aero FEA Engineer** - Looks at the structural integrity of the car. Update specifications based on the study of linear and non-linear structural analysis of vehicle structure, and components.
- **Mechanical Aerodynamics Design Engineer** - Will optimise the mechanical design and minimise weight of the carbon lay up and release drawings.
- **Junior Aerodynamic Design Engineer** - Prepare scale wind tunnel models, run and analyse wind tunnel tests to maximise downforce, you will be looking for about 2500kg of aerodynamic downforce with minimal drag.
- **Aerodynamist -Track Side Support** - Are responsible to de-

termine the aerodynamic set up based on driver feedback and monitors the live data during sessions and diagnosis of aerodynamic issues.

- **Track Aerodynamicist** - Reports feedback and post analysis of track activities to help drive the development cycle.
- **Aerodynamic Applications Engineer** - Works on the design of experiments in the wind tunnel and creates specification for software to support visualization or analysis tools.

Full scale aerodynamic testing must be carried out at an FIA approved test track and is limited to 5 days per year. Therefore the teams carry out testing in a wind tunnel.

WIND TUNNEL ENGINEERING

The wind tunnel is a laboratory for experiments with a large fan that simulates travelling at speed through the air. Models of the car are placed in the tunnel and some facilities may use streams of sulfur hexafluoride and nitrogen to create the white lines you see stream over the models.

Financial fair play rulings limit the amount of aerodynamic wind tunnel testing that can take place. The FIA reserve the right to visit and inspect factories at any time during the season.

Teams can use no more than one wind tunnel to conduct testing and must be able to prove it can be calibrated for a maximum wind speed 50m/sec or 111.85mph / 180.00kmh for F1 testing. The models must be a maximum of 60 percent scale, and only 1 model can be used in a wind tunnel test. The maximum amount of testing to be conducted is 80 runs and 60 hours occupancy in the tunnel in a week. This ensures all teams have the same amount of access and opportunity to optimise the aerodynamic performance of the car.

Full details of wind tunnel test requirements can be found in the F1 sporting regulations. These can be viewed via the **www.jobsinf1.com** technical pages.

- **Wind Tunnel Model Manager** - Books the facility and agrees the tests to be carried out by engineering. They then run the test to conditions agreed and record the data with high speed cameras and video cameras.
- **Junior Aerodynamicists** - Will assist in the set up of the model in the laboratory and review and analyse the test set up and results to achieve a better aerodynamic performance.
- **Wind Tunnel Technician** - Is responsible for test set up and maintenance of the facility. Ensures model quality and accuracy at all times and tests the model parts and assemblies in line with the current wind tunnel schedule.

R&D DYNAMICIST ENGINEERS

An in depth knowledge of vehicle testing techniques and experience in the design of experiments for whole vehicle testing is required. Knowledge of simulation systems like Matlab/Simulink and SIMPACK benefit these roles helps to correlate real world results with actual test data.

- **Head of Vehicle Dynamics** - Oversees all dynamic development by working alongside the race & test teams, and the design office where science and simulation lead the design evolution. Working alongside the race and vehicle science teams they apply their experience of limit handling, tyre modelling and performance assessment in a racing environment to deliver optimum vehicle performance through the application of various modelling methodologies and analysis techniques.
- **Vertical Dynamicist** - Uses a 7-post shaker rig to mimic the dynamic loads that will be subjected to the car. Telemetry data is collected from the cars for each track and this is used to simulate each racetrack. The car is then subjected to multiple lap simulations and engineers study every aspect of the cars designs, performance and durability. Data is collected, analysed and used to improve R&D design and testing methods. They prepare reports and inform the design engineering team of the results.

- **Senior Vehicle Dynamic Engineer** - Runs simulation programmes. This is theoretical engineering purity based on mathematics and physics. Complex models and algorithms compute a theoretical lap and how the car interacts with the track. The data can be correlated to actual data captured from a race or test. The design and set up of the car can be tuned to close the gap between theory and actual data. Determines the set up of the car based on feedback from the driver and data analytics and experience.

- **Vehicle Dynamic Development Engineer** - Analyses and predicts vehicle and systems performance primarily looking at mechanical solutions, such as suspension components, springs, dampers and brakes. Will study the telemetry data and optimise vehicle set up.

- **Vehicle Dynamics CAE Engineer** - Specialises in vehicle dynamics simulation. This includes the integration of breaking and slip control systems, torque vectoring and aerodynamics to optimise the chassis and vehicle systems performance.

MATERIALS ENGINEER

Is usually a specialist in carbon fibre but also researches new materials, process and technology for all materials with the aim of minimising weight and increasing material strength and stiffness. Builds test samples and validates the performance. Maintains a database of approved materials and their characteristics, and confirms IMDS (International Materials Database System) registration.

MECHANICAL DESIGN ENGINEER

Specifies the requirements and mechanical loads, and designs all kinds of moving mechanical components and rigid parts for the key vehicle systems of the car. This is a great place to learn vehicle integration and understand how the whole car works. It involves mainly design work and creating drawings to high precision/tight tolerance design. Most of the time is based in the design office.

Tools used for design & simulation include CATIA V5, MATLAB/ Simulink, Mathworks, ALIAS, Siemens NX (formally Uni-Graphics).

All components on the car have a mechanical design modelled to verify their package, kinematic movement and weight.

POWERTRAIN

- **Head of Powertrain Engineer** - Specifies the requirements for the whole powertrain, including engine, transmission, clutch, differentials and control systems. All development engine & powertrain build requirements have to be agreed with the suppliers and a plan created to support continuous development. Leads extensive liaison with supply chain management and suppliers to plan & deliver test bench & vehicle based engine & powertrain builds including parts availability and readiness for build and test.

- **Powertrain Simulation Engineer** - Runs CAE simulation to test each part of the powertrain, every component needs to be tested beyond its limits. They simulates lap drive cycles that take the powertrain up and down the rev range, simulate gearshifts, braking and all loads that the vehicle will be subjected to on the track. Material operating temperatures are measured, oil and cooling fluid temperatures and pressures are checked, and airflow through the car is monitored.

- **Powertrain Co-Coordinator** - Maintains the bill of materials, orders parts and books stock into the development environment. Ensures robust plans are developed and executed in order to successfully build, test and develop powertrains using test rigs, dynomometers and in vehicles testing.

ENGINE

- **Head of Engine** - Determines the engine specification based on the FIA rules for the season. In 2014 a major change to engine capacity and configuration was introduced moving to a 1.6L turbocharged V6, revving to 15,000 rpm to produce about 600bhp with additional power provided by energy recovery systems, so engine development for the start of the 2014 season is critical for the coming seasons.

Develops the integration concept of the engine to the vehicle because the engine forms part of the structure of the car and the rear suspension mounts to the engine and gearbox assembly. Defines the engine performance limits, control strategy and test requirements.

Most of the engine development and testing takes place at the engine supplier and this can be read about a little further through the book.

- **Senior Powertrain Engineer** - Has to maximise the available power from the configuration and rules. Ensures smooth and consistent power and torque can be delivered. Uses CAE and simulation to tune the engine performance and design requirement. Studies design tolerances, materials characteristics and coefficient to ensure compression is maintained through the performance range.
- **Powertrain Design Engineer** - Designs the integration of the engine and powertrain package into the vehicle using 3D CAD models. Experienced in a test and development environment – test set up, instrumentation, logging, fault analysis, data processing and reporting.
- **Engine Test Technician** - Maintains the laboratory and installs the engines to the test bed. Sets the test screen parameters for each test scenario or drive cycle, records the data and prepares reports. Adjusts engine parameters using the engine management system (EMS) and monitors the effects on engine operation, emissions and power.

COOLING SYSTEMS

Cooling System Engineer - Cooling of the car is reliant on airflow, F1 cars do not have cooling fans and this is why portable fans are used to keep the car cool on the grid and in the garage. The system comprises of a header tank with a pressure release blow off valve, radiators, cooling hoses, couplings and pump. The engineer needs to vary the bodywork and ducting to cope with the varying climates and temperatures experienced by the car. There are many changes that occur to the cooling system in a season due to the different circuits and their environment.

FUEL SYSTEMS

Fuel Systems Engineer - Designs the fuel tank, fuel pump, hoses and couplings. Uses CFD to minimise turbulence of fluid and ensure smooth and consistent deliverance of the fuel and air ratio. Teams used to be able to use unlimited fuel and would consume about 160kg per race, but from 2014 will be restricted to 100kg per race.

EXHAUST

The exhaust is designed by a powertrain engineer to move the exhaust gases quickly from the engine but minimise the package size to suit the aerodynamics. Gases are used to power the turbine for the turbocharger and the exit of the tailpipe must be angled upwards to prevent the exhaust flow being used for aerodynamic effect. Bodywork cannot be placed behind the tailpipe. So the designer needs to meet the requirements of the engine manufacturer and the aerodynamic team.

TURBOCHARGER (TC)

Designed by a powertrain engineer the turbocharger is a forced air induction system that puts more air and a higher proportion of fuel into the combustion chamber and makes the engine more powerful and efficient. Powered by a turbine that is driven by the exhaust gases it can suffer a lag from engine rpm to turbine rpm. The engineer needs to tune out that characteristic using CFD modelling.

TRANSMISSION

- **Head of Gearbox** - Responsible for the technical management and delivery of a 7 speed forward and 1 reverse gear transmission and rear impact structure in carbon fibre. Development includes torsional vibration damping strategies, driveshaft system, and control system development and calibration.

- **Mechanical Design Engineer Transmission** - Calculates the drive gear ratios and stresses that will be exerted on the gearbox, selects gear oil to reduce fluid traction losses, designs a compact gearbox that can pre-prime the clutch for gearshift before the driver selects it.

  Experienced in data analysis, data mining and signal processing and writing data manipulation software in AutoiT and data analysis scripts in MATLAB.

- **Gear Box Technician** - Manufactures gearbox components using CNC machine tools, Electro discharge machining (EDM), profile gear grinding, worm thread grinding and gear cutting machines. Assembles the transmission and tests it on a rig.

- **Transmission Dynomometer Engineer** - Runs the dynamometer tests within a climatic wind tunnel including a rolling road rig to accommodate a range of gear ratios and to run in the mechanical components in the whole powertrain.

  The engine needs to be started via a shaft that exits the back of the transmission, to do this a high torque motor with a reduction gearbox paired to a portable high power battery.

ELECTRIC POWERTRAIN

Electric Motor & Generator

Electric Machines and Drives Specialist - Develops the specification and design of the permanent magnet electric motor (Motor Generator Unit-Kinetic MGU-K) using modelling simulations in PSpice and Matlab/Simulink/Stateflow to optimise the performance of magnetic field and windings. Calculates energy performance and tunes the gap between peak and continuous power output of the electric motor. Develops the embedded control system, and analogue/digital circuit design using Cadence Orcad to integrate with the power inverters and converters. Specifies the algorithm and calibration for the controller power electronics. The motor generator unit-heat (MGU-H) is an electrical machine linked to the exhaust turbine of a pressure charging system as part of the energy recovery system (ERS).

Energy Store (ES)

Battery Systems Engineer - ESS Engineers use iPSpice and Matlab/Simulink/Stateflow for modelling and simulation of the battery systems and to put them through circuit simulation cycles. Develops the high voltage battery ESS (energy storage systems) >12Vdc <1200Vdc and BMS (battery management systems), sizes cables and busbars, contactors and fuses, and all elements of the electrical and electronics and cooling systems. EMC mitigation, control strategy and thermal management are key to optimising performance. Designs the control experiments for HIL & SIL tests and on battery packs, diagnoses faults, provides technical liaison with component suppliers, technical support for commissioning and integration of the storage system into the application. Cell chemistries used in electric/hybrid electric vehicle batteries are usually Lithium Ion based, but each team will chose its own exact chemistry. The ESS will give the drivers about 160bhp for approximately 33 seconds a lap.

The car also carries a 12V Lithium Ion battery charged by an alternator to run the electronics.

CHASSIS ENGINEERS

The chassis is made up of the chassis structure and the chassis systems that mount to the structure. Engineers use CATIA V5, CAE and MATLAB/Simulink to develop the chassis and chassis systems. The driver needs to understand the characteristics of the chassis to feel the behaviour and adapt his style to suit the car.

Structure

- **Senior Chassis Engineer** - Responsible for specifying the chassis dynamics, including suspension brakes, pedals, wheels and tyres with the vehicle dynamics team. Establishes the requirements specified by the FIA for dimensions, safety and roll hoop structure. Sets the functional targets and loads for static and dynamic stiffness, crash requirements, the passive safety survival cell and the fuel tank housing behind the driver. Defines the strategy for joining processes such as mechanical fastenings and bonding, and manufacturing processes for casting and composites construction.

- **Lead Chassis Designer** - Responsible for design and development of all chassis system and components, develops technical solutions to assist the production and manufacturing engineers. Uses CAD to shape the chassis, creates drawings and technical notes to support the manufacture of the chassis.
- **Chassis Engineer** - Specifies the testing requirements for the roll structure, side impact and squeeze test to prove out the safety survival cell. Will work with the chassis designer to increase the strength of the chassis using FEA stress analysis to improve the design. Will conduct the tests on chassis in laboratories for dynamic and crash validation.

SIMULATION ENGINEERS

For design & simulation - CATIA V5, MATLAB/Simulink, Mathworks. Siemens NX7.5 or higher tools are used.

- **Head of Stress Section** - Creates and monitors methodology that is applied to FEA analysis within the design office, proof tests and signs off procedures and reports.
- **Structural Engineer** - Specialises in component design, including stiffness and strength performance, fatigue and an understanding of joints such as bolted, bonded and welding using FEA and CAE tools for pre/post processing and problem solving.
- **Stress Engineer** - Carries out structural analysis of the components. This will be using both finite elements and hand calculations. Based in the design office to ensure components released to production meet the set strength, stiffness and mass requirements and specifies tests. Reports the analysis from testing to allow the engineering drawings to be approved by the Head of Stress department.
- **FEA Engineer** (Finite Element Analysis) - Is ideally a mathematical modeller with a scientific and engineering knowledge. Develops the test model and analyses components for potential failures. Assists the designers with data that describes the potential failures that could occur so that they can be engineered out.

- **Simulator Modelling Engineer** - Develops race simulation scenario models. Creates the model mesh over the geometric parts and enters the material property parameters. Specifies the test conditions and environmental conditions for each track.
- **Simulator Test Engineer** - Runs the simulation tests. Monitors the simulation parameters, trials different parameters scenarios, and carries out post-test analysis and writes reports.
- **Team Leader Powertrain Simulation** - Analyses the performance of the complete drivetrain and integration to the chassis and chassis systems.

HYDRAULIC SYSTEM ENGINEERS

- **Hydraulics Group Leader** - Specifies the requirements for the engine driven hydraulic pump, actuators and the high-pressure accumulator, hose routing and chassis systems. Brakes are also hydraulic but form part of a separate system.
- **CFD Hydraulic Engineer** - Carries out computational analysis of the hydraulic systems fluid dynamics and designs an integrated high-pressure hydraulic system. The engine crankshaft drives the hydraulic pump and the fluids can be switched and moved to support the systems on the car like the power steering, throttle, clutch & gearshift and differential. The brakes are a separate hydraulic system, and the engine may use electro hydraulic engine valves.
- **Junior Engineer Hydraulics** - Contributes to the design of the hydraulic system. Prepares and carries out testing on hydraulic systems, monitors system performance, adjusts test parameters and records data for analysis.
- **Hydraulics Development Technician** - Builds and maintains rigs and fixtures suitable for testing and development of hydraulic components and assemblies, including in-life servicing of components.

SUSPENSION ENGINEER

Suspension Design Engineer - F1 suspension only moves a few millimetres so it is important to get the minimum ground clearance right and minimise effect to aerodynamics, ensure stiffness of the components and limit the motion of un-sprung mass on the car. Designs the upper & lower wishbones, push/pullrods, uprights, anti roll bars, torsion bars, dampers, heave spring, anti roll bar links. The suspension needs to minimise weight transfer due to lateral and jacking forces. Extended tyre wear can occur if the suspension pitches and rolls.

STEERING ENGINEER

Steering Design Engineer - Designs the steering column, universal joint, power assisted steering (PAS), and the track rods. Low speed understeer is a common problem for an F1 car so the driver needs to tune the system to work with the suspension, wheels and tyres and aerodynamics.

STEERING WHEEL ENGINEERS

Mechanical & Electronic Engineers - The steering wheel is a complex ECU unit used to steer the car. It has a carbon fibre structure containing the mechanical mountings for the steering column and quick release lever as well as the mechanical buttons for selecting or adjusting functions, the gear shift paddles and the internal electronics. The steering wheel is therefore a system developed by mechanical and electronic engineers, and therefore is a man machine interface (MMI), the designer needs to factor the ergonomics of the driver, and shape the wheel to the grip of the driver's hand, reducing any stress or strain to the drivers grip and wrist, reducing fatigue. The driver also needs to be able to see and adjust all of the dials or press the buttons whilst wearing gloves and driving the car, so the positioning of all this functionality needs to be within the dexterity range of the drivers hand movements. The less time the driver needs to look at the steering wheel the more time he has to optimise his lap.

The steering wheel displays the speed of the car, the gear, and the drivers position in the race, and the row of LED's display the rpm of the engine in green amber and red indicating the optimum time to shift up or down. FIA flags used trackside by marshals and race control lights are also displayed in the car.

Controls on the steering wheel are used to:

- Select neutral gear,
- Paddles shift up & down gear,
- A button to select reverse gear,
- Inform the team the car will be pitting,
- Enable & disable the pit lane limiter,
- Confirm or cancel a setting selected by the driver,
- Adjust front wing angles,
- Adjust fuel mix,

- Adjust engine performance,
- Transfer oil from a reserve tank,
- Select weather conditions to adjust the vehicle settings,
- Enable and disable ERS and adjust setting,
- To Initiate and disable DRS,
- A button for the warm up lap by adjusting settings for maximum wheel spin,
- Adjust brake balance,
- Initiate pit radio
- Provide a drink to the driver

PEDALS ENGINEER

Pedal Design Engineer - The pedal assembly is made up of the pedals, linkages and master cylinders and mounting plate. The throttle is linked to an electronic throttle sensor (potentiometer) that controls the demand for fuel via an FIA approved ECU.

The brake pedal is linked to the hydraulic system for slowing the car. There is no clutch pedal, the clutch is controlled electronically by the steering wheel paddles and ECU that can pre-prime the clutch.

BRAKES ENGINEER

Brake Design Engineer - Responsible for the whole brake system although calipers and discs may be supplied from a specialist company the Brake Design Engineer needs to specify the requirement. Due to the high temperature created a ceramic carbon compound is used to cope with temperature. The designer needs to integrate fluid reservoirs, discs, calipers, pads, hoses, brake pedal, master slave cylinders, brake bias lever (that adjusts the balance of the brakes) and linkages and the cooling ducting and shrouding on to the car. The system operates hydraulically but also has electronics and uses infra-red temperature and wear sensors. Since the introduction of ERS the teams can use an electronic rear brake control system as a result of the extra power being generated under braking by the energy recovery system, so the engineers now need to factor if the energy recovered should be used as additional power source or for braking. A dynamometer test is carried out to validate the performance of the system.

WHEEL ENGINEER

Chassis Systems Engineer & Wheel Supplier - The dimensions of the wheel are specified by the FIA but the design and composition of the wheel is the responsibility of the chassis systems engineer. The wheel is a structural component but needs to be lightweight, so the engineer needs to determine the correct material properties for the loads and temperatures. The wheel needs to disperse heat generated by the brakes so needs a flow of air entering through the ducting on the inside of the wheel and dispersing outside the wheel causing minimum effect to the aerodynamic flow of the car. The wheel engineer works closely with the tyre partner to ensure good sealing surfaces. The wheel requires CFD analysis to refine the shape and depth of the spokes.

TYRE ENGINEERING

Senior Tyre Design Engineer & Chassis Systems Engineer - A manufacturing partner designs and supplies the tyres, and the manufacturing process is a closely guarded secret. But the tyre falls into the responsibility of the chassis systems team. The whole chassis and chassis systems needs to be engineered as a package to work in harmony. So developing the car is a partnership between the tyre manufacturer and the systems engineers, and the effect of the tyre under certain operating conditions needs to be disseminated to the whole car development team.

Tyres come in various compounds to suit each race climate and conditions. The compounds are soft, medium, hard, intermediate wet and full wet race tyres. The soft medium and hard tyres are slicks, this means they have no tread and this maximises the surface contact to the track for better grip. A slick tyre on a wet track aquaplanes like a boat and has little grip, so the intermediate and full wet tyres need a tread to pick up and direct water away from the contact area to the track and disperse the water to the sides. The design of the water management is done using CFD simulation and physical testing. The tyre is a rubber based chemical composition overlaid on a lightweight nylon and polyester fibre ply structure, so the engineer needs a chemical engineering and or a mechanical engineering degree. Due to the cross plies weave structure it has the characteristic to creep along the strands when a lateral force is applied, this can be predicted and this is why you have handed tyres on the car.

The toughest part of tyre development is being able to understand how the tyre changes its characteristics during a race. The effects of heating and cooling down, the lateral forces constantly changing create a fluid movement of the surface rubber, this ever changing grip wears as the friction from the surface of the track peels the surface off the tyre. Over the course of the race making the transitions occur quicker due to the reduced amount of material.

Grip is affected heavily by the amount of aerodynamic downforce and the lateral G's that are applied by cornering, and longitudinal forces applied under accelerating braking. The teams now use infra-red sensors to learn how the tyre temperature and surface area alters and this data will be converted into a simulation model for each circuit, and then run as a module in the complete vehicle race simulation.

BODYWORK ENGINEER

Composites Lead Engineer – Shapes the bodywork and works closely with the stress and aerodynamics teams to ensure that the body will stand up to the aerodynamic load & downforce, as well as the mechanical loads. Ensures that manufacturing is able to produce each panel consistently and to specification. They specify the type of ply used and the orientation of the lay up to meet the structural requirement.

SOFTWARE ENGINEERS

Writes the embedded code that operates on the electronic units, and application software.

F1 teams use many types of software. Ideally you should have a Mechanical Engineering or Computer Science degree with experience in the following software:

For design & simulation - CATIA V5, MATLAB/Simulink, Mathworks.

Object orientated programming in C+, C++, Python, Java, NET, Visual Studio, Linux.

Web page development - HTML5, JavaScript, Django, Dojo or other framework.

User interface design and development - QtCreator and QtDesigner.

The companies have the core team of people but several contractors may be used.

- **Senior Software Engineer** - Will gather the company requirements and oversee the software development. Determines the SIL test requirements from concerns raised in the DFMEA and tests the software so that every potential failure has a corrective action or failure mitigation control.
- **Senior Control System Track Support Engineer** - Provides track support for the configuring of the car set up, monitoring performance and diagnosis of on-car electronic control systems and tools.
- **Control Systems Development Engineer** - Creates real-time embedded application software models for high performance ECU's.
- **HPC Engineer** - Develops the High Performance Computing cluster that is used for in depth analysis from multiple systems, allowing the user to overview the complete vehicles performance and interaction of systems.
- **Software Test Engineer** - Validates Real Time Embedded Software that controls and monitors the cars health according the to the SIL requirements.
- **Senior Software Developers** - Creates the simulation and analysis tools for the vehicles dynamic systems. Develops the complex algorithm code to correlate data taken from the telemetry system on the car, into the simulator program.
- **Simulator Technician** - Will programme the simulation parame-

ters. Tests the software's robustness on the simulator. Maintains the simulators in an operational state.

- **CFD Web Development Engineer** - Designs the tools using Python / PHP / MYSQL / Javascript / Data Mining for the purpose of aerodynamic modelling.
- **Aerodynamics Software Programmer** - Develops computational tools for the aerodynamics team.
- **Software Engineer** - Support multiple contract software requirements.
- **Application Developer** - Develops user administration tools for company personnel.

ELECTRICAL ENGINEERS

Designs the wire harness and EDS electrical distribution system to MIL (military) standard, lays out the schematic drawing for the vehicle and designs the pin-to-pin connections from the electronic control units. Vehicle communications and function are a result of this integration. The engineer needs to overcome the challenge of EMC (electro magnetic compatibility) that can disrupt communications. Specifies how the wire harness needs to be assembled and tested.

Knowledge of electronics design tools like ORCAD, mechanical design tools like CATIA V5 and Vesys that covers PCB design, schematic and harnesses linked to 3D data are favourable, and knowledge of MIL (Military) specification wiring installations is essential.

Head of Electrical Design - Determines the schematic architecture layout of the car to deliver electronic and electrical systems integration, and to minimise the weight of the harnesses.

Electrical Engineer - An EDS (electrical distribution system) engineer designs the race car wire harness for 12V and HV systems. They take a 3D virtual design and develop it into fully engineered vehicle electrical systems and circuits, creating drawings that detail manufacturing requirements and installation instructions.

ELECTRONIC ENGINEERS

Specifies the requirements of electronic functionality. Designs the hardware and PCB layout, selects the components and defines the firmware and software requirements. Builds and tests the prototypes. A good degree in Electrical/Electronics Engineering is needed and knowledge of analogue and digital circuit design and high speed data acquisition is essential.

Knowledge of electronics design tools like ORCAD and mechanical design tools like CATIA V5 are favourable as well as knowledge of MIL (Military) specification wiring installations sensor technologies and standard electronic test equipment. Familiarity with shaker rig testing, harness testing equipment and data acquisition software would be beneficial.

- **Head of Electronics** - Specifies the requirements of the integrated systems. Approves HIL (Hardware in Loop) and SIL (Systems in Loop) testing results and releases the units for use on the car.
- **Electronics Design Engineer** - Designs the hardware of the VCU (Vehicle Control Unit) & peripheral CPU (Central Processing Unit) modules. Mocks-up the electronic units and designs the experiments. Defines the analogue/digital circuit design using Cadence Orcad to integrate with the vehicle systems and simulates vehicle robustness with HIL & SIL testing. A software engineer develops the embedded systems and control system algorithm and calibration parameters.

  Two other systems fall into this role, the rear rain light and the umbilical.

  A small battery system is carried on the vehicle, but this cannot sustain the car over the course of the day, an auxiliary power supply is attached and this is known as the umbilical. This also carries data from the car to download and monitor the cars health.
- **Electronics Test & Inspection Technician** - Develops testing equipment and processes. Tests the robustness of the

wiring harness and electronics on the shaker rig and verifies functionality and software data acquisition.

- **Power Systems Engineer** - Designs power electronic converters and propulsion systems using simulation to model power electronic conversion and performance analysis. Develop electrical and electronic components and systems, and manages cost and manufacturing quality.
- **Telemetry Engineer** - A telemetry module is a device that receives and stores data that can be transmitted via a mobile telecom link. This is how the pit wall and headquarters receive streams of live data from the car. The engineer is a specialist electronics engineer in data communications, storage and management. They specify the requirements for data to be captured from key systems on the car, and create a strategy that ensures data is held incase the communications link is broken, and then transmitted or downloaded from the car at the first opportunity.
- **Data Logging Engineer** - Data logging means capturing the data files from the cars ECU's so that the teams can analyse the health of the car and pick up data from sensors to aid development. The sensors monitor temperature, many of the moving parts and the ride height so the engineer needs to determine where on the car they need to be located to collect the information required for development, but also for the FIA accident data recorder. The data is either transmitted by the telematics system or saved to a memory storage device.
- **Radio Systems Engineer** - The driver wears a radio microphone and in ear headsets to communicate with the pit wall. To talk the driver presses a button mounted on the steering wheel. All communications are monitored by the FIA but are encrypted so that other teams cannot listen to the transmission. The signal is transmitted from an aerial usually mounted in front of the cockpit. This means that the radio is likely to survive an accident and communication maintained.

  The radio engineer also develops a timing transponder that

emits a unique identifying radio signal that responds to an interrogating signal received from under the racetrack at the sector gates. This is used to measure the position and lap times by sector.

- **Race & Test Engineer** - Attends all of the races, analyses telemetry data and works with the driver and race engineer to suggest ways to change the set-up of the car in qualifying, in a bid to eliminate any potential problems during the race before a failure occurs on the car. In depth knowledge of the whole car and methodical attention to detail is required to run simulations based on previous races or test session.

MECHANICS

Mechanics not only build and maintain the cars but they provide the engineers with great insight in to how to design for assembly and service, they witness any potential stress failure crack, torque relaxation or mechanical problem first hand and the mechanics are an important part of the design team.

- **No1 Mechanic** - Attends all races and track test to make sure the cars are built and maintained exactly as designed, drawn and specified by the design office. Monitors the pit stops and responds quickly to any problem. To become a No1 you need knowledge and experience either in F1 or have held the position in another team or similar formula and be used to working under pressure to tight deadlines.
- **No2 Mechanic** - Supports the No1 Mechanic but has the primary responsibility to build the car in the factory before it is shipped to test or race. Works with and oversees the sub-assembly mechanics and raises build issues with the design office. Assembles cars for rig testing and works on mock ups of the car and assemblies.
- **Race Team Mechanics** - Carry out the mechanical work on the cars in the pit garage, ensure the cars health and temperature is managed, and make up a majority of the pit stop crew. They travel with the car to testing and support No1 & No2 mechanics.

- **Sub Assembly Mechanic** - Pre-assembles components into sub-assemblies using jigs and fixtures to assemble and test parts before they are installed on the vehicle.
- **Garage Technician** - Provides support to the race mechanics and maintains the equipment and tools. Learns first hand how the cars are built, maintained and set up.

RACE TEAM

The teams may take anywhere between 60 and 100 people to a Grand Prix, depending on the race event, the planned business negotiations and the size of the budget.

- CEO
- Team Principle
- Technical Director
- Drivers 3-4
- Chief Financial Officer
- Head of Communications
- Press Officer
- Sponsorship Manager
- Head of Vehicle Dynamics
- Head of Aerodynamics & CFD
- Head of Powertrain
- Head of Research & Development
- Head of Race Strategy
- Team Manager
- Chief Engineer
- Chief Designer
- Controls Engineer Race Support

- Race Engineer x 4-6
- No1 Mechanic & Garage Mechanics x 20-25
- Tyre Technicians x2
- Radio Technician
- Personal Trainers x2
- Physiotherapist x2
- Truckie x 25-35
- Team Kit Manager
- Head of Hospitality
- Hospitality Staff x 5-10
- Chef x2
- Kitchen Assistance x2
- Logistic Manager
- Head of Merchandising
- Lawyer

BACK AT HEADQUARTERS

Race Strategy Team

Head of Race Simulation – Leads the team that predicts the outcome of the team's race before a wheel has been turned. Provides statistical data to the team principle to help support the race strategy and when the pit stops will occur.

Mission Control x12 – Run the simulation before and during the race. Continually update and adjust parameters based on race events and competitor positions.

KEY SUPPLIERS

Like many industries, F1 requires suppliers in order to provide components and services. You can look at a number of these external organisations as a means to gain experience and prove you have the right education and experience to support a career in F1.

So, for example, you could look at the engine, transmission, brakes, ESS Battery, wheels and tyre suppliers. Not many F1 teams make their own powertrain components and you will generally find that a specialist company produces them.

This kind of company will provide great experience for any mechanical, electrical or electronic engineer. You will be able to witness the development of the specification, design, assembly, the preparation of test requirements and validation of these parts, and post test data analysis and problem resolution before they are prepared for shipping. And this is all fantastic knowledge, so that when you approach an F1 company you can explain to them exactly how their component is prepared and demonstrate how to ensure the quality and robustness of the hardware, firmware and software. That in depth knowledge explained during an interview is very impressive to the people that are conducting the interview.

So, it's definitely worthwhile having a look at the components, the major components that are used on a F1 vehicle, and just simply using the internet as a means to search for companies that specialise in producing those components. Any company that is associated to an F1 will quite happily brand and display their logos or list those F1 companies as being somebody that they supply to, to demonstrate the quality of their parts.

Engineers with experience in chemical engineering, materials engineering, electrical and electronics, software and control systems, hydraulics, mechanical and manufacturing process all contribute to the development of these key systems.

You can obtain a list of suppliers from **www.jobsinf1.com.**

ENGINE SUPPLIER

- **Engine Design Engineer** - The engine supplier may supply several teams but each customer might have slightly different specification and test requirements. They read the specification regulations from the FIA and work with the teams to deliver an engine to their requirement. They design the engine with the required displacement and minimum aerodynamic package, simulate the engines performance and characteristics by using FEA, CAE and CFD techniques, produce tooling to manufacture parts for assembly.
- **Engine Builders** - This is a meticulous and precision skilled individual that builds the engine to a process and includes polishing the cylinder block and pistons, cams, valves and push rods, crankshaft, to ensure the precision fit, reduce friction and energy loss. Usually working with another builder so that they can build sub-assembly part and checks each other's work. They are mechanical artists with no room for error. Each engine takes approximately two weeks to build and will be tested on a dynamometer to check the power output.
- **Engine Validation Technician** - Each engine will be subjected to start up and shut down, warm up, hot and cold starts, rig testing, compression, torque and power testing, rpm stability, rpm tip in & tip out, vibration, noise, emissions, varying orientation drive cycles, climatic and environmental performance, cooling, oil consumption, fuel consumption, water ingress, general reliability and high speed testing to name a few tests. Once the full performance of the engine has been proven it can be prepared for delivery. Approximately 70 individual tests are carried out and provide data for a significant number of post analysis tests and simulations.
- **Supporting The Customer** - The engine supplier will support the customer with a race support engineer at all of the test and race events. They will be expected to analyse engine data, respond to any issue that occurs and ensure the control systems operate correctly.

TRANSMISSION SUPPLIER

Transmission Designer - Housing, gears, shafts, pins and actuator controls go through a similar development, manufacturing and validation process to the engine and will also be put through a number of unique characteristic and environmental tests.

Transmission Test Engineer

The gearbox would be subjected to engine start and stop, launch and consecutive gear shifts, shift quality at extreme temperatures, ratio evaluation and friction loss assessment, gear whine, gear rattle, idle rattle, engine bending torsion, bearing life, shunt rig load reversals, constant run peak torque, racing engine, slipping lock up and clutch drive, clutch static stall testing to name a few. Approximately 65 types of tests are carried out on the transmission.

BRAKES SUPPLIER

Brake System Engineer - The principles of designing a disc brake system is very well tried and tested. A significant proportion of the development is in understanding the attributes of how the system performs and this means a lot of testing is required. Materials technology is a major part of the development for the disc and brake pad compounds. This is to create the right braking performance and feel as well as standing up to the extreme operating temperatures.

Brake System Test Engineer - Braking feel, grab, fade, lane stability, yaw response, brake in turn stability, deceleration response and performance in all environmental conditions, pulsation, durability, longitudinal disturbances during braking, noise, vibration, brake pedal feel hysteresis are a few of the tests carried out.

Engineers with experience in chemical engineering, materials engineering, electrical and electronics, software and control systems, hydraulics, mechanical and manufacturing process all contribute to the development of this system.

ESS SUPPLIER

Developing an energy storage system is a complex product requiring specialist expertise. It is a high density and high power Lithium Ion battery.

The control and failsafe systems are critical to ensure that the battery systems and the chemical composition stay within the optimum operation window. Each and every control action must have a control plan to covers every potential eventuality. It must also continually watchdog and mitigate any potential failure, and a time triggered intelligence operating in milliseconds. The system should also have an isolator and switching contactors to kill the circuits. The whole system should comply with the ISO26262 standard.

Due to the combination of high and low voltages in the systems, mitigating EMC is a major factor. The different electromagnetic frequencies can cause interference that distorts the messages being transmitted and received by the ECU's, with the potential of causing unintentional operation.

The system will be put through a significant amount of low voltage testing and short circuit and ground fault detection testing, ripple and quiescent current tests. The charging capability, battery capacity, efficiency and discharge rate all need to be verified, as well as several mechanical factors and its resistance to water ingress and impact.

TYRE SUPPLIER

The FIA & teams agree on a tyre supplier for the season and F1 is a special division of the tyre supplier providing support at all events. The teams do not develop tyres. Internal development is continuous throughout the season, any issues raised by the teams or the FIA need to be extensively investigated.

PERIPHERAL BUSINESS

The F1 teams do not travel alone, they are accompanied by a wide range of individuals and companies that are licensed either by the FIA or the promoter to support and promote the sport.

MEDIA

The media plays a major role in F1, without it the only way you would get to see an F1 race would be to attend in person, and that would only be if someone told you personally that it was happening. So what does the media do in F1?

The race and circuit promoters will use the media to publicise the race event and sponsor, and this will be advertised on television, the Internet, newspapers and billboards, magazines and motor racing clubs. There are several job opportunities that exist in media, and the basic level of media support involved in an F1 promotion event is:

- Race Promotion Manager
- Lawyers
- Financiers & Buyers
- Sponsors
- TV Presenters, Pundits, Drivers, Team Principles, Mechanics.
- TV Crew Camera Men, Light Men & Sound Men, Pilots & Drivers.
- Technical Specialists for IT & Broadcast
- Models, Stylists & Wardrobe, Make-Up Specialists
- Photographers
- Journalists
- Website Admin
- Printers
- Publishers
- Support from Race Team PR & Media Crew
- Race Team Mechanics & Team Drivers
- Track Officials
- Safety Officers
- Club Secretaries
- Medical Teams (depending on event)

FOM

Formula One Management are the media company that transmits on board footage. The cameras are assembled to the car during the build process. This data captured on car is streamed via the telematics unit and broadcast by FOM around the world under license. They also visit the team headquarters to film special features and interviews or PR material on behalf of the teams.

TV Presenters & Pundits

These are the people at the front of the media coverage that provide an insight into the sport. Presenters are usually a former member of an F1 team or a trained TV journalist.

Photographers

Teams of journalists and photographers follow all events from practice sessions, Grand Prix race weekend preparations & set up and race event and after party activities, capturing the story of the event and the people and places. The world press and media will buy or use the pictures under license.

Journalists

National and local press as well as magazines and TV all need articles and blogs written for publishing. Interviews need to be conducted and research carried out to verify facts. Freelance journalists are paid by the story and often have to fund their own travel.

TROPHY DESIGN & MANUFACTURE

Each race has a unique trophy awarded for 1st, 2nd and 3rd place as well as for the winning constructor. Each trophy needs to be designed and will be manufactured using precious metals by a jeweller.

CHAMPAGNE SPONSOR

The champagne spray is one of the most iconic images captured on film. G.H.Mumm is the champagne sponsor to F1.

F1 LOGISTICS

DHL have been the recent supplier that supports transporting F1 and their tools and equipment when road journeys are not an option.

This is managed as a special division of the company. Planners, ground co-ordinators, pilots, forklift drivers, material handlers, couriers in cars and vans, truck drivers, motorcyclists have to ensure everything arrives on time.

INSURANCE

Insuring an F1 company and all of its travel and logistics requires special expertise. Much of the equipment is unique and hugely expensive. When something goes wrong there is a very small window of opportunity between races to fix the issue.

PERFORMANCE SCIENCE

A performance scientist assesses the physiological and biomechanical performance of an athlete as well as cognitive intellectual and thinking capabilities. They study existing methodology & practices and apply scientific principles to aid the technique and movement, as well as ensure nutrition and adequate rest and regenerative activities support the athletes well being.

PRINTING COMPANIES & PUBLISHERS

There are several companies that produce race programmes and motorsport magazines, merchandise catalogues, collector photographs and pictures.

COACH BUILDERS

The trucks and the hospitality units need to be designed and built. In some cases the units can cost millions of pounds and are as technically impressive as any part of the cars. Many of the trailers are like huge transformer toys kitted out with technology and comfort and takes a team of truckies to prepare them for use at each race. The vehicles go through a significant amount of vehicle and equipment testing before the teams accept delivery.

MERCHANDISE MANUFACTURERS & RETAILERS

F1 merchandise is a huge business. Each team has its own branded products produced under license and this includes clothing to key rings and even broken parts of cars after an accident.

TICKET AGENTS

The sale of F1 tickets and hospitality packages ranges from standing areas, grandstand seats and various packages all the way to helicopter flights with hospitality and pit lane passes, camping or 5 star hotels. To explore the types of packages offered visit **www.jobsinf1.com** and view our Grand Prix tickets page.

ORGANISATIONS & CLUB ADMINISTRATION

Supporting or working for the FIA, BRDCC, BRDC, MSA, ARD's & ARK's will help you to build your network and knowledge of the motorsport industry. Some are full time occupations and others require voluntary services to manage their affairs.

The FIA have many specialists that support the Grand Prix including the FIA President, Race Director & Official Starter, Operations Team, Rescue Co-Ordinator, Safety Car Driver, Medical Car Driver, Medical Delegates, Technical Representatives, Communications Team, Software Analysts.

SPONSORS

A Sponsor may be in any kind of global business, the teams look to capture brands that are recognised and located worldwide. You can look to work in the sponsor's organisations with a focus to PR and marketing as an option.

RECYCLING & WASTE MANAGEMENT

F1 has been criticised for damaging the environment but recycling is a side that not many people are aware even takes place. F1 has always been at the pinnacle of technical performance and manufacturing but it also works hard to limit its impact on the environment and helps to innovate recycling technologies and works with suppliers to develop processes that support the global demand.

MANUFACTURING EQUIPMENT

Equipment suppliers for automation technologies like CNC machines and lathes, hand tools and electronic devices. These machines need to be maintained and serviced frequently, then calibrated to ensure that accuracy in production is maintained.

RACE CLOTHING & EQUIPMENT

Race clothing is usually sponsored and needs to be designed to suit the brand and sponsorship contracts. All clothing must meet the FIA requirements.

CHAUFFEUR'S

Not only do chauffeur's take the drivers and team principles to the circuit they serve another important function. In some parts of the world pedestrians will throw themselves in front of a car in the hope of an accident payday, especially if the driver is famous. The chauffeur protects the driver and the team from prosecution and insurance claims.

HOTELS

When the teams travel hotels are prime candidates for a large booking as teams and fans all make their arrangements. Owning a luxury hotel near a Grand Prix circuit can be rewarding.

TRAVEL AGENTS

F1 has been known to draw up to 400,000 visitors at a race event, 30,000 people may camp and a large proportion need to arrange their travel package.

16. THE JOBS IN F1 WEBSITE

The website was set up to provide on going support for buyers of the book. If you have not already done so visit **www.Jobsinf1.com** and subscribe as a member.

There is information that you need access to help you establish your career, and it changes on a regular basis, we cannot update published books but we do offer that service on the internet in the members area.

By becoming a member it helps us keep you informed of new information and updates on the website, and by joining our Facebook, Google +, Twitter and LinkedIn pages, you will receive free updates and newsletters that will keep you up to date of the latest jobs and vacancies within F1, as well as interesting facts and F1 news.

For a bit of fun we run a competition where you can win the current season's F1 winning car as a 1/18 scale model. This is a fantastic prize for any F1 fan and is a collectable item. In order to win you need to subscribe to the **www.jobsinf1.com** website. The prize will be drawn annually on the last day of the F1 season.

Member's Area

The information in this area is only available to members. It is published online rather than in this book so that it can be updated and kept relevant. Two levels of membership are offered, Grid & Podium.

Grid membership is free to join and a few of the benefits of membership are:

- Free admission to the 1/18 scale model competition,
- Access to technical information and recommended books,
- How a Formula 1 car is designed and built,
- Grand Prix tickets & hospitality can be purchased,
- F1 merchandise and gifts can be purchased,

- Periodical special information features.

Podium membership is for professional career development.

For An Engineer

- Available Jobs In F1, notifications, news and updates,
- How to write a CV and review service,
- Companies used for recruitment,
- Educational information for future F1 engineers,
- Who Works In F1.

For A Driver

- Driver Career Development Information
- List of sponsors,
- List of suppliers,
- Driver management.

You can submit your CV to Jobs in F1 and we maintain a database dedicated to people interested in a career in F1.

Forum

We have an F1 forum blog dedicated to F1 fans where you can add your experience and tips that will help the next generation of sports fans become a F1 team member.

Merchandise

Interview Support Products - We offer products that support preparation for your interview. You can video your habits and record your audio presentation as explained in this book.

Games - To help keep things fun we have an F1 games page, this is to help you learn about the circuits and how to set up an F1 car for a race through playing games.

Watches - Like many technical people we have a passion for watches and if you like to keep good time and keep up to date with the latest

F1 fashions, you can purchase official sponsor F1 watches via the website. Jobs In F1 has gone to a great deal of effort to create this collection of F1 watches and a good watch will only impress at an interview.

We have a page dedicated to watching F1 on mobile devices and interactive apps to download, so you will also be able to keep up to date with F1 races and details of the teams and race calendar.

17. CIRCUITS & VOLUNTEERS

VOLUNTEERS

Race circuits are operated and run by specialists in PR, event management consortiums and national racing clubs. There are several different events that take place at a circuit over a race season; this can be anything from hosting a Grand Prix weekend, to club events and public track days. Most circuits now have their own driving schools or allow access to corporate entertaining and track days. For all of these events, circuits require stewards to patrol the circuit and the pit lane and this can be an opportunity for volunteers to get involved in motorsport and to get close to the race teams as they prepare over the weekend. There are different sources of information on becoming a marshal and this can help you get involved as a timekeeper, a technical official or a track side steward and having a disability doesn't stop you being involved. You could even consider working in one of the driving schools to gain experience as a steppingstone in your career. The MSA has some guidance at **Volunteers In Motorsport**, the BARC has advice at **BARC Marshaling**, and you will also need to become a member of the British Motorsport Marshal Club at **BMMC Marshal**.

UK RACE CIRCUITS

The UK based circuits where you could look to marshal are:

- Abingdon Airfield, near Abingdon in Oxfordshire
- Angelsey in North Wales
- Bedford Autodrome, near Thurleigh in Bedfordshire
- Blyton Park, near Gainsborough in Lincolnshire
- Brands Hatch, near Dartford in Kent
- Bruntingthorpe, near Lutterworth in Leicestershire
- Cadwell Park near Louth in Lincolnshire
- Castle Coombe, near Chippenham in Wiltshire

- Chobham Test Track, Chertsey in Surrey
- Croft, near Catterick in North Yorkshire
- Donington Park, near Castle Donington in Derbyshire
- Elvington, RAF Elvington in Yorkshire
- Goodwood near Chichester in West Sussex
- Great Tew Estate, Chipping Norton in Oxon
- Heyford, Bicester in Oxon
- Hullavington, Chippenham in Wiltshire
- Jurby on the Isle of Man
- Kenilworth in Warwickshire
- Knockhill, near Dunfirmline in Fife
- Llandow in Glamorgan,
- Lydden Hill, near Canterbury in Kent
- Mallory Park, near Hinckley in Leicestershire
- Mondello Park, Donore, Naas in Co Kildare
- Oulten Park near Tarporley in Cheshire
- Pembrey, near Llanelli in South Wales
- Rockingham, near Corby in Northamptonshire
- Silverstone, near Towcester in Northamptonshire
- Snetterton, near Norwich in Norfolk
- Thruxton, near Andover in Hampshire
- Top Gear – Dunsfold Park, Near Cranleigh in Surrey

Contact details can be found in the member's area at:
www.jobsinf1.com

FORMULA 1 CIRCUITS

The F1 circus is a nomadic event and travels the globe visiting between 18-20 circuits. If you are planning an F1 career you have to be prepared to travel with it and not be at home for several weeks at a time. You have to be prepared to work in the uncomfortable climatic environment, and learn to abide by the customs and laws of these countries. You may be required to declare any medication or even consider vaccinations if you wish to travel. Many teams provide catering services but if you are not prepared to eat local food you may not enjoy the experience of travel.

A typical F1 season looks like the following:

- 14-16 Mar - Albert Park – Melbourne – Australia
- 28-30 Mar - Sepang International Circuit – Kuala Lumpar – Malaysia
- 4-6 Apr – Bahrain International Circuit – Sakhir - Bahrain
- 18-20 Apr - Shanghai International Circuit – Shanghai – China
- 09-11 May - Circuit de Catalunya – Catalunya – Spain
- 23-25 May - Monte Carlo – Monaco
- 06-08 Jun - Circuit de Gilles Villeneuve – Montreal – Canada
- 20-22 Jun – Red Bull Ring – Spielberg - Austria
- 04-06 Jul - Silverstone Circuit – Silverstone – Britain
- 18-20 Jul - Hockenheimring – Hockenheim – Germany
- 25-27 Jul - Hungaroring – Budapest – Hungary
- 22-24 Aug - Circuit de Spa Francorchamps – Belgium
- 05-07 Sep - Autodromo Nazionale di Monza – Monza – Italy
- 19-21 Sep - Marina Bay Street Circuit – Singapore – Singapore
- 03-05 Oct – Suzuka Circuit – Suzuka – Japan
- 10-12 Oct - Sochi International Street Circuit – Sochi - Russia

- 24-26 Oct - Circuit of the Americas – Austin – USA
- 07-09 Nov - Autodrome José Carlos Pace – Sao Paulo – Brasil
- 21-23 Nov - Yas Marina Circuit – Yas Marina – Abu Dhabi

In recent years F1 has also visited:

Jaypee International Circuit – New Delphi – India.

Korea International Circuit – Yeongam - Korea

Other circuits that were under discussion but have not yet been selected are:

Autódromo Hermanos Rodríguez – Mexico City – Mexico

Port Imperial Street Circuit – New Jersey – USA

18. HOW TO BECOME A FORMULA 1 DRIVER

There are five recognised routes to developing your driving career.

The first is based on raw talent and determination to succeed and this means developing your skill and progressing through the formulas.

The second is to pay to drive and this is usually the reserve of teams in the lower end of the grid that need a substantial cash injection to support their season. In today's market the price of a seat is believed to be about five million pounds.

The third is to pick-up a sponsorship deal and be the preferred driver for that brand, this also means a significant cash injection for the team.

The fourth is to drive for an engine manufacturer, with partnerships between teams and engine manufacturers a driver can be included as part of the deal. The list of engine suppliers to F1 changes from year to year as each team negotiates new deals and regulation changes mean new engine requirements and layout configuration changes, or as new teams enter or leave the F1 circus. The current short list of engine suppliers is:

1. Ferrari
2. Renault Sport
3. Mercedes AMG HPP
4. Cosworth
5. Honda
6. Toyota
7. BMW
8. Illmor

The fifth is to be enrolled by a team offering a "Young Driver Programme". In order to be considered you will need to have a proven record of performing well in Karts or lower single seat formula. McLaren were the first team to take this initiative and Lewis Hamilton is the living proof of the success of this sponsored route.

Many of todays F1 drivers use a combination of raw talent and one of the other means to negotiate their progression in to Formula 1. A talented driver will attract sponsorship throughout their racing career. Most drivers start by creating their own team, and running their own car until they are invited to join a bigger team or can expand their own team with sponsorship.

With sponsorship a driver can earn a good income to support the development of their cars as they move through the formulas. Sponsors also provide a selection of parts or services to assist a driver and this significantly increases the viability of a team to finish the season with funds for next years season.

Once a driver has demonstrated their talent they will attract the attention of a larger team with better funding. With a professionally prepared and maintained car it will help you to put your car at the front of the grid and increases your chances of winning a championship. If you want to be an F1 driver you have to win championships or consistently be on the podium.

Before we get too far ahead of ourselves we need to start to explore how much talent and commitment a driver has and how they can afford to pay for a career in motorsport.

SPONSORSHIP

Finding a willing sponsor to give you cash to fund your racing career can be a challenge, even if it is your parents. Most children and teenagers may understand the concept of how money buys things but may not have a full appreciation of how much effort is required to earn the disposable income required to fund racing, most people only make enough money to cover the household bills. Any experienced racer will tell you "don't go racing with your own money".

The other challenge is that your parents will have to start finding time in their busy lives to drive you around the country to attend all of the race events, just turning up to support the race weekend costs entrance fees, hotels, fuel, food and this is all after you have bought your car and paid for it to be converted to a race car, bought the basic spares, and a trailer to tow your car to the track, and the all expensive tool box and tool kit. You also need somewhere to work on your car; this could be your garage, a marquee on the driveway or a workshop. The bottom line is this all costs money, so where will you get the money?

A sponsor will want advertising space on your kart, car or racing overalls. They may also want to receive free entrance tickets for hospitality so that they can entertain their clients, as an entrant you may receive tickets for each event that you can pass on to your sponsor. They may want you to promote their business by attending events with your car, or doing interviews for the radio or TV to promote their product or service. Always remember that sponsorship is a business deal to which both parties look to find mutual ground for their own benefit.

In return they may offer you products or discounts on items from their stores like tools and equipment, fluids, or they may offer you services like car preparation, these are great support for any young driver but you cannot beat the flexibility of cash. You should look to try and negotiate some cash in each deal.

The first place to look is local auto garages, auto spare shops and car dealerships, these are all good place to start if you are competing in a one make series like Formula Ford, at least they have an interest in your make of car as a foundation of their business.

Secondly who currently sponsors race teams in your formula? They will already have an idea of what they can offer in terms of finance and what they expect to get back in return. They may not be prepared to renew sponsorship on an existing team or driver, especially if you are performing better than their driver.

You can also obtain a list of potential sponsors from the member's area at **www.jobsinf1.com.** These companies have an association to F1 so may have the potential to sponsor your entire career.

Before you go and ask for sponsorship have a good idea of what you need for the season ahead. Look at the finance of the entry fees and the costs to turn up at each circuit. Consider the consumable items on the car like tyres and brakes and pads. Look at what is in danger of damage from a crash and think about a sensible number of spare parts.

Do not rely on just one sponsorship deal, any one sponsor should not make up more than 25% of your budget, this is incase your sponsor goes bust or cannot pay their part of the sponsorship deal. It is easier to replace a small portion of your budget than the complete seasons finances, especially if you have fronted any expense from your own pocket.

When you are setting your annual budget you need to assign an advertising cost to each visual part of your car, this is best calculated by percentage of budget required. The prime locations are the side pods, engine cover, rear wing, front wing, nose cone top and then nose cone side. Tyres always display the manufacturers name so look to get sponsorship from them based on your formula supplier.

Your race suit and helmet are also good for sponsorship and the head and shoulders are visible in the car or during an interview and always feature in pictures.

The best way to get a sponsorship is to use driver management. We explain driver management later in the book but these are professional and experienced individuals with a large number of contacts.

You could also contact the Racing Steps Foundation (RSF), this organisation provides support and backs drivers in the lower formulas of racing from Karting into Formula Renault, Formula 3 which may at its discretion continue through a young drivers career. There are also successful teams associated to the RSF; they are Zip Young Guns, Carlin Motorsport and Fortec Motorsport.

Visit **Racing Steps** for further details.

19. KARTING

HOW TO GET STARTED

If you are planning on becoming a Kart or Race Car driver your first point of reference should be the Motor Sport Association. The **MSA** govern motorsport in the UK.

The usual route for people to enter into motorsport is to start off in Karting, and there are several different Formulas of Kart. You can compete in junior and cadet levels, before moving on to take part in senior events and progressing up through the 125cc, and the 250cc categories.

Your starting point is to purchase the MSA Go Karting Starter Pack at **MSA Karting Starter Pack.**

You can attend a Kart school to gain your first experience by contacting the Association of Racing Kart Schools. To arrange your training visit **ARKS.**

Karting formulas for young drivers are:

- MSA Bambino (6-8 Years)
- MSA British Cadet Kart Championship (8-13 Years)
- MSA British Junior Kart Championship (11-16 Years)
- MSA British Short Circuit Championship (16+ Years)
- MSA British Long Circuit (Superkart) Championship (16+ Years)

Details of these formulas can be found at:

- Getting Started In Karting
- British Superkart
- The Association of British Kart Clubs has a full description of Kart formulas and requirements.

KARTING KIT & EQUIPMENT

Two trusted sources for Karting kit and equipment are Zip Kart at Zip Kart and Grand Prix Racewear at GP Direct for your clothing requirements. There are several other sources you can choose, but these are among the best.

All Clothing must conform to FIA 8856-2000 regulation. Read about it at **FIA Clothing Regulations.**

Another option open to you is to buy your rolling chassis and then participate in the Superone Mini Max & Junior Max Academy. Entry fees, engine hire, tyres, fuel, oil are all included in the fixed fee package. Visit **Superone Series** for further details.

20. BECOMING A RACING DRIVER

BECOMING A RACING DRIVER

When somebody wants to become a racing car driver they need to be over the age of 16. It is a requirement for the Association of Racing Drivers test to be taken, this is also known as the ARDs test. And this is the basic level to show that you understand track protocol, have competence to drive and control a vehicle on a racetrack, and that you understand the motorsport flag systems, and that you have learnt how to conduct yourself on a circuit and not be a danger to other drivers. This is both a practical and an academic test, and to pass the test is a requirement to be able to drive on any circuit in the UK. Your starting point is to purchase the MSA Go Racing Starter Pack at **MSA Go Racing Starter Pack**. You can arrange your ARD's test by applying to the schools approved by the Motorsport Association (MSA) at the **Association Of Racing Drivers Schools.**

You do not need a medical for your ARD's test but you will need a medical when you apply for your National B License. A medical check and certificate costs about £60 and takes about 20 minutes at your local doctors surgery but the MSA does have a list of recommended doctors.

LICENSES

The progression through licenses is to start with a National B Licence, then progressing to an International B Licence, National A License and then an International A License; these can be applied for at **License Applications**. To become an F1 driver you need to progress another level and hold the FIA F1 Super license. We explain this later in the book.

BRIDGING THE GAP FROM KARTING TO RACING AGES 14-16

FIESTA JUNIOR

Once you have passed your ARD's test you can enter the Fiesta Junior series that is affiliated to the BRSCC & MSA. This is ideal for those young drivers aged 14-16 years to progress to a hatch back sized vehicle from Karts. The driving experience is significantly different to driving a kart. The car has suspension where a kart uses the chassis as its means to suspend the vehicle. Other dynamics of pitch, roll, yaw, power and the size and mass of vehicle will help a young driver to sharpen their skill and become familiar with the characteristics of over-steer and under-steer and car to car contact.

To compete in this series you can either buy your own Fiesta ST to prepare and race, or you can buy the "arrive and drive seat" with one of the teams. Excluding the initial purchase cost of the car you could run your car for the season for about £8,000 or you can buy a seat for about £16,000, however some of the bigger teams may request up to £30,000. Talent is the true winner at this level, not budget. The season consists of 16 races over 8 weekends comprising of practice and qualifying on the Saturday and two races on the Sunday.

Fiesta Junior Championship is administered by the BRSCC.

Visit: **Fiesta Junior** for further details and advice.

What you will notice as you move from a saloon car to a single seat race car is that you would have developed your awareness of vehicle dynamics in a vehicle that exaggerates those characteristics to a greater extent than that of what you will experience in a single seat race car.

ZIP FORMULA

Once you have passed your ARD's test you can enter Zip Formula. This is a single seat formula and was set up to give drivers aged 15 years or over a level technical playing field to prove their talent, although it does carry a fee of circa £30,000 for a single years racing. For further information visit **Zip Formula.**

You should now look to join

The British Racing & Sports Car Club (BRSCC)

The British Racing Drivers Club (BRDC)

The British Automobile Racing Club (BARC)

These organisations provide a wealth of information and oversee several formulas and events and manage UK based racetracks. The BRSCC's blue ribbon event is the Formula Ford Festival that takes place a Brands Hatch every October, for any aspiring driver this is an event to have your talent recognised and is a key steppingstone on the route to F1.

21. ROUTE TO A FORMULA 1 SEAT

CHOOSING YOUR CAREER PATH

Not all formula have a direct route to F1 so you have to choose your route to F1 based on your opportunities. The following research is based on the 2013 & 2014 F1 driver's routes to their seat.

The formulas recognised as providing a direct seat to F1 are: GP2, GP3, Formula 3, Formula 3000, Formula Renault 3.5, Although one World Champion made the jump from Formula Renault 2.0 as a double champion in to F1.

F1 Seat Approach Funnel

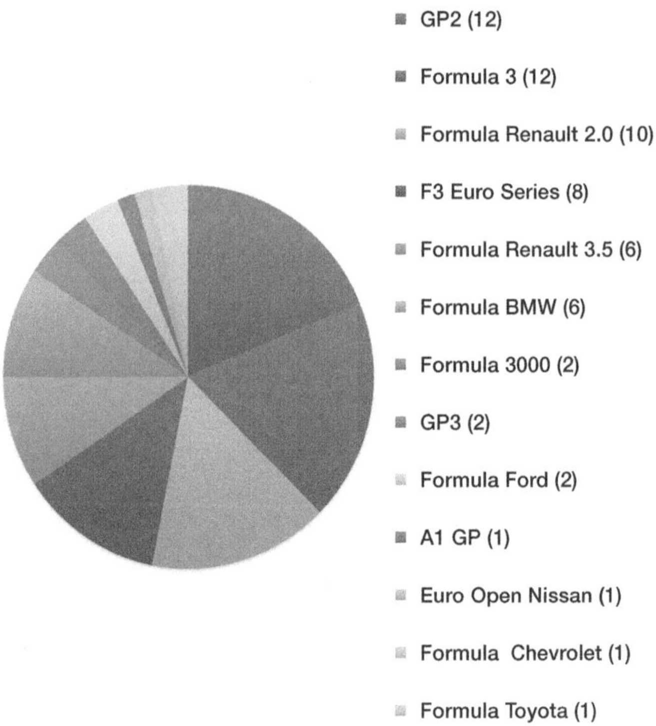

Final Move To An F1 Seat

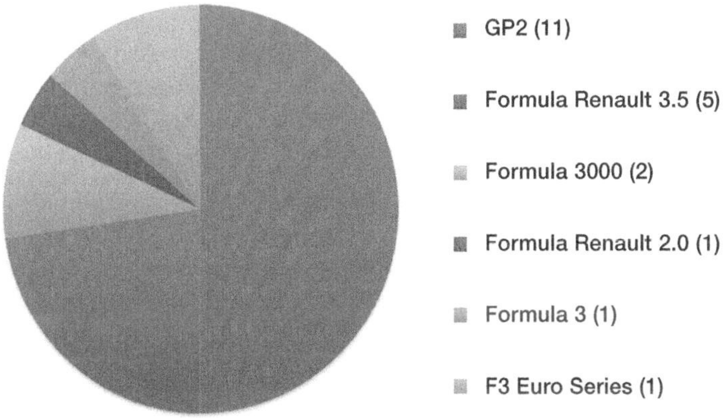

The peripheral steppingstone formulas are: Formula Ford, Formula Renault 2.0, Formula BMW, Formula Chevrolet, Euro Open by Nissan, F3 Euro Series, Formula 2, A1 GP. These formula have been used by the drivers holding an F1 seat in 2014, but they are by no means the only peripheral formulas in which you can gain experience. The most important thing you need to do is to perform well, perform consistently, and being podium placed.

A few things to consider are the fact that GP2 replaced Formula 3000 in 2005 and that Bernie Ecclestone and Flavio Briatore own the rights to the GP2 Series. The significance of this is that GP2 is a support race that competes on the F1 weekends and benefits from TV coverage and access to sponsors and media. Drivers also have the opportunity to network with the F1 teams. Formula Renault 3.5 also makes an appearance on some F1 weekends.

GP3 was launched in 2010 as a feeder formula to GP2, and you can see that the recent younger drivers are progressing from GP3 through GP2 and into F1.

Not only do you need talent and sponsorship, you have to learn the politics of F1.

Most drivers start in karting, and then move to the bridging formulas and then the peripheral racing formulas before moving into the final approach funnel. Many drivers may compete in more than one series in a season or enter special events, but a common thread of core Formula appears in all cases and this is what I call the approach funnel. Even if they participate in an academy programme to build their career, they still follow this route. The examples of the main-stream approach funnel routes taken to F1 for the drivers is as follows:

RED BULL

Vettel → F3 Euro Series → Formula Renault 3.5 → *F1*

Ricciardo → Formula BMW → Formula Renault 2.0 → Formula 3 → Formula Renault 3.5 → *F1*

MERCEDES GP

Hamilton → Formula Renault 2.0 → F3 Euro series → GP2 → *F1*

Rosberg → Formula BMW → F3 Euro series → GP2 → *F1*

FERRARI

Alonso → Euro Open Nissan → Formula 3000 → *F1*

Raikkonen → Formula Renault 2.0 → *F1*

MCLAREN

Button → Formula Ford → Formula 3 → *F1*

Magnussen → Formula Ford → Formula Renault 2.0 → Formula 3 → Formula Renault 3.5 → *F1*

LOTUS

Grosjean → Formula Renault 2.0 → F3 Euro series → GP2 → *F1*

Maldonado → Formula Renault 2.0 → Formula Renault 3.5 → GP2 → *F1*

FORCE INDIA

Hulkenburg → Formula BMW → Formula 3 → A1 GP → F3 Euro series → GP2 → ***F1***

Perez → Formula 3 → GP2 → ***F1***

TORO ROSSO

Vergne → Formula BMW → Formula Renault 2.0 → Formula 3 → Formula Renault 3.5 → ***F1***

Kvyat → Formula Renault 2.0 → GP3 → F3 Euro series → ***F1***

WILLIAMS

Massa → Formula Chevrolet → Formula 3000 → ***F1***

Bottas → F3 Euro series → GP3 → ***F1***

MARUSSIA

Bianchi → Formula Renault 2.0 → Formula 3 → GP2 → Formula Renault 3.5 → ***F1***

Chilton → Formula 3 → GP2 → ***F1***

CATERHAM

Kobayashi → Formula Toyota → Formula Renault 2.0 → Formula 3 → GP2 → ***F1***

Ericsson → Formula BMW → Formula 3 → GP2 → ***F1***

SAUBER

Sutil → Formula 3 → GP2 → ***F1***

Gulierrez → Formula BMW → F3 Euro series → GP3 → GP2 → ***F1***

There are of course exceptions to the rule but they will have proven significant talent in some of the above and many other formula.

Formula Renault takes place as a national event but there are also continent wide competitions. In order to gain maximum exposure you should look to compete at both levels.

SUPER LICENSE

Before you can compete in Formula One you have to qualify by virtue of progressing your driving career and ability to the point where you can attain the FIA F1 Driver Super License.

The FIA Sporting Regulations state the following:

5.1 Qualifications

5.1.1 must be the holder of a current FIA International Grade A license.

5.1.2 must also satisfy at least one of the following requirements:

a) You must have made at least 5 starts in races counting for the FIA Formula One World Championship for Drivers the previous year, or at least 15 starts within the previous 3 years.

b) You have previously held the Super Licence and have been the regular test driver with a Formula One World Championship team for the previous year.

c) You have been classified, within the previous 2 years, in the first 3 of the final classification of: the F2 Championship, or the International F3 Trophy, or the GP2 Series, or the GP2 Asia Series or the Japanese F/Nippon Championship,

d) You have been classified in the first 4 of the final classification of the Indy car IRL series within the previous 2 years,

e) If you are the current champion of one of the following:

- Formula 3 Euro Series
- The principal national F3 championships of: Great Britain, Italy, Japan, Spain
- World Series F/Renault V6

N.B.: the title of Champion is considered valid for 12 months from the last race of the relevant series or championship season.

f) The driver judged by the FIA to have consistently demonstrated outstanding ability in single-seater formula cars, but with no opportunity to qualify under any of c) to e) above. In this case the Formula One team concerned must show that the applicant has driven at least 300 km in a current Formula One car consistently at racing speeds, over a maximum period of 2 days, completed not more than 90 days prior to the application and certified by the ASN of the country in which the test took place.

5.2 Application Procedure For FIA Formula One Driver Super Licence

a) The complete application must be received by the FIA at least 14 days before scrutineering for the first FIA Formula One World Championship event in which the candidate is to compete. In the case of a driver change in the Championship for reasons of force majeure, the FIA may accept applications up to 48 hours before the start of initial scrutineering for the event.

b) The ASN, which issued the driver's current competition licence must submit to the FIA a specific recommendation, accompanied by the driver's record of results and current International A licence number.

c) The driver must submit a completed Super Licence application form to the FIA.

d) The annual Super Licence fee must be paid to the FIA.

5.3 Conditions of issue For FIA Formula One Driver Super Licence

5.3.1 When Articles 5.1 and 5.2 have been complied with to the satisfaction of the FIA, it will issue the licence.

5.3.2 The Super Licence will be valid to the end of the year of issue.

5.3.3 A driver accepted under the terms of 5.1.2 f) above will be on probation for a period of 12 months during which the Super Licence will be held provisionally and subject to review at any time.

5.3.4 A driver will remain eligible for the renewal of a first Super Licence for 8 months after the date of issue, subject to compliance with 5.2 b) to d) above.

(Source – FIA Sporting Regulations section 5.1 to 5.3.4)

Super License Fees

The FIA charge an annual flat fee of £10,000, plus £1000 for every point the driver accrues over the season. So a driver needs to factor his license fee cost in to his pay and sponsorship deal.

It is not a requirement but many drivers do join the Grand Prix Drivers Association (GPDA). This costs about £2000 to join and is where the drivers and test drivers can discuss issues like driver safety.

The next question to be asked at this point is how do you get to drive in these formulas? If you have the funds yourself, family that are willing to pay, or you have big enough sponsorship deal to fund your career, you can buy a drive. If you don't have the above you need Driver Management.

DRIVER MANAGEMENT

Once you have completed your ARD's test you should begin to think about getting a manager.

What will a manager do for you?

Firstly you are going to need someone with experience of negotiating a contract with the teams and the sponsors. They need to ensure there is enough money left in the deal for a good level of pay for the driver. Because an agent takes a commission it is in their interest to ensure a good financial deal.

The agent will make sure you hold the right license for the formula to which you intend to race. Without the right license you will be refused race entry at scrutineering.

The agent is also expected to raise your profile as a racing driver, and possibly negotiate the number one seat in the team, or have a seat promotion clause should an existing number one driver leave.

A manager may have a portfolio of sponsors to take to the negotiating table but some teams like to control which sponsor's are on their cars, charging a premium to existing sponsors for the exclusivity of the marketing potential from the car. If the drivers personal sponsors are to be excluded from the teams branding the driver may lose his personal sponsor, if this is the case the driver should request a higher retainer fee to compensate for the loss of income from a sponsor.

Aside from the commercial responsibility they manage the relationship between the driver and the team, this helps to keep the day-to-day working relationship clean and allows the driver to focus on the job of driving and developing the car.

Keeping the driver in the right frame of mind is essential to succeeding in F1. A driver may need a PA to organise PR events, a physical trainer, a dietician and a chef, all these people need to be organised and keeping the driver in a routine as much as possible given the travel and time zones experienced in the F1 season.

The bigger and more successful driver managers obviously cost a significant amount of money. A list of agents associated to F1 can be found in the member's area at **www.jobsinf1.com.**

FORMULA 1 JUNIOR TEAMS

Some of the F1 teams run their own academy for young drivers, the first team to initiate a driver development programme was McLaren and the result was Lewis Hamilton. These sponsorships are offered based on continued hard work, achieving good grades at school and because a modern F1 driver needs to be every bit an engineer as the team around him; you must achieve success on the track or you will not be considered as a viable candidate until you have a racing pedigree and can demonstrate you have achieved a championship podium finish. If accepted this becomes a sponsored drive with the focus on becoming an F1 driver, and also includes a significant amount of training in driving, behavior, public relations, safety, principles of fair play and sportsmanship as well as being put onto their fitness programme.

McLaren - Young Driver Programme

Ferrari Driver Academy

Lotus - Junior Team

RedBull - Junior Team

Caterham Team Academy

Marussia Young Driver Program

Mercedes - Young Star Driver Program

Force India Team Academy

Williams may be in the process of forming a young driver programme.

Toro Rosso is associated to the RedBull Junior Team

Sauber support the FIA Young Driver Academy.

F1 Junior drivers will be put through the key formulas mentioned in Route to F1 chapter to prove their capability just like any other driver.

THE FIA INSTITUTE FOR YOUNG DRIVER EXCELLENCE ACADEMY

As well as F1 teams the FIA takes not only driver development very seriously, but also offers you an opportunity to contribute to the future of motorsport and be instrumental in rule and legislative changes. They also offer training programmes in safety, medical excellence, fitness and psychology, public relations, publications on motorsport safety, and you can contribute to research projects investigating driver safety. Participation in these events can deliver you a place on the academy.

The Young Driver Excellence Academy offers training to a global audience with Europe, Middle East, Africa, Americas, and Asia Pacific offering a sponsored route into motorsport, and is a full education programme as well as driver training, visit The **FIA Young Driver Excellence Academy** for further information.

THE MSA YOUNG DRIVER PROGRAMME

The MSA also run a National Academy called **MSA Academy**, follow the link for full details.

THE BRDC YOUNG DRIVER PROGRAMME

The BRDC encourages talent and has its own training programme called **BRDC Superstars** . Follow the link for full details.

DRIVER PAY & RACE BUDGETS

Many people ask how a drivers pay is structured and how much does a racing driver earn? This varies from team to team but estimates of agents, managers and teams lead to the following:

A drivers' income is between 40% to 70% retainer and 30% to 60% bonus, based on podiums, wins and championship position. If you look at where you expect to finish in your formula you can adjust this guide on a pro-rata basis. You also have to be realistic when setting your budget for your race season and invest some time thinking about what the season will cost. You need to be sure that your sponsor has the finances should you exceed expectation. A driver may at their discretion share some of the bonus with the team members if they pick up a podium.

The costs for Kart racing can be kept relatively sensible and within a family budget from £2000 to £6000, but moving up the ladder and competing in the lower driver formulas will cost £15,000 - £30,000 to run your season, you will also need consider earning a living and some disposable salary.

As you move up the formula into a season in the peripheral formulas you need to think about either building a team and getting a manager or becoming part of an established team. Whichever route you choose you need to work on the following scales of budget :

Your vehicle is likely to be a minimum of 30% of your annual budget.

Karting = £2000 - £6000

Fiesta Junior = £8000 - £30,000

Zip Formula = £30,000

Formula Ford = £50,000 - £100,000

Formula Two = £200,000 - £250,000

Formula BMW = £250,000 - £300,000

Formula Renault 2.0 = £300,000 - £350,000

Formula 3 = £350,000 - £400,000

F3 Euro Series = £500,000 - £600,000

GP3 = £500,000 - £600,000

Formula Renault 3.5 = £700,000 - £750,000

GP2 = £1,500,000 - £2,200,000

F1 = £5,000,000 - £35,000,000

Dependent on driver's ability and reputation the retainer for an F1 driver could be between £3.5 million to £15 million a season with the cost being shared by the team and sponsors. The drivers earning increases based on wins and podium finishes, and a driver with personal sponsorship or advertising deals could earn another few million for the season.

The financial cost cutting measures imposed on the sport and with the recession we have seen the retainer costs reduced in recent years. With the financial reward being driven towards bonuses and the demands for points and position, the drivers agent also needs to negotiate severance packages if the driver's seat is cut during the contract, some sponsors have significant financial muscle and it's not always financially viable for a team to ignore a willing sponsor.

TECHNICAL INSIGHT

It is important for everyone to get a technical insight into car design, the development process and the build and manufacturing process of the car. Understanding how the car is constructed and in what sequence is essential for any design engineer to understand how to design the car for manufacture.

It's also very important to gain a general understanding of the design concepts, and particularly in relation to aerodynamics. This is very similar to the principle of the butterfly effect where one small event or change can have a heavy impact on something somewhere else on the vehicle, and you have to understand and appreciate this to design for the package and not just design for the component. You have to understand the characteristics of your vehicle and of your components, to evaluate the material properties, the mechanical movement, the forces the car is subjected to and the effect of the environment in which it operates.

To gain the understanding of these principles, there is no substitute for education, and I would definitely recommend reading at least one book that characterises each of the key factors of an F1 car.

Visit the technical pages in the members section at www.jobsinf1.com for further details on the F1 rules and regulations, car design, how a car is built, recommended reading titles that give you an insight into engineering the major systems of an F1 car.

Formula 1 Teams Family Tree

The two most successful teams in Formula one are Ferrari & McLaren, they also happen to be the two teams that have competed in F1 the longest. Over the years many teams have come and gone and the current family tree shows how teams have changed ownership.

Many of the teams have changed ownership since their conception. Championship winning teams no longer exist in some cases, and it is interesting to see how some team names end and then re-emerge replacing another team as owners wrangle for team names and brands, set up new partnerships and build on the development of a teams design.

The history of the teams:

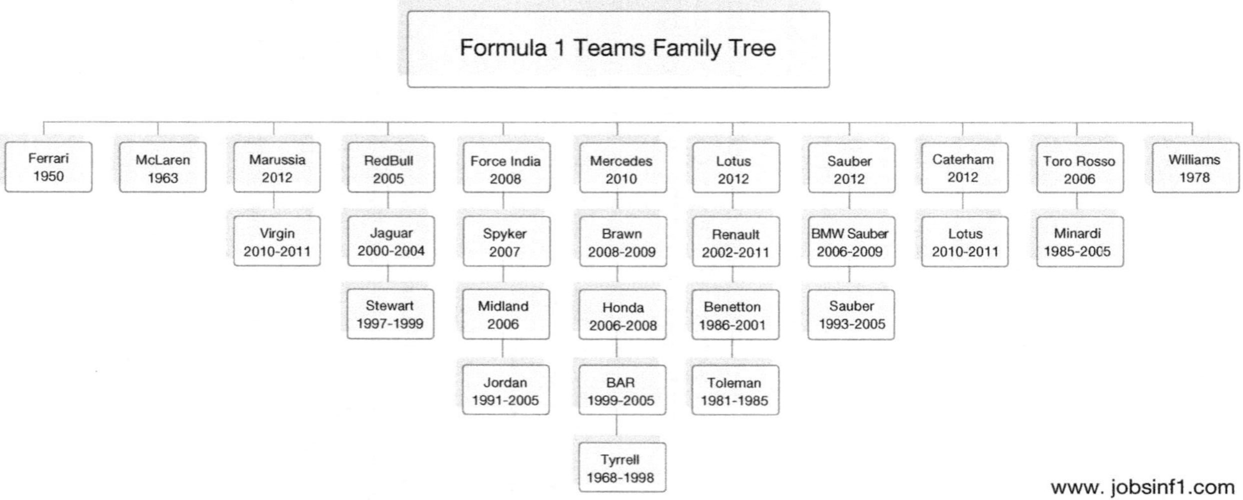

www. jobsinf1.com

22. PREPARING FOR RACE WEEKEND

Logistic Planners

The logistics team have to do a significant amount of planning to ensure that every detail of the logistic chain has been covered, that all paperwork is in order so that nothing is held up at customs. The cars must be drained of all fluids before they can be transported. Each piece of kit is put in a box, logged and confirmed before the trucks are loaded. Each container is meticulously loaded placing everything on the truck to support the unpacking and garage preparation sequence at the race venue.

Truck Drivers

A single team will likely have 3-6 trucks at a race weekend with two drivers per vehicle. The vehicles are used for transporting cars, tools and equipment, and the hospitality trucks. There are also the driver's own personal trailers in which they relax and prepare themselves for the race.

The truck drivers carrying the cars will be the last of the transporters to leave headquarters so the cars can pick up as many late updates as possible. Like any member of the team the drivers keep their kit meticulously clean and washing that huge truck one of the first jobs to be done before they leave and when they arrive. Some of these trucks cost millions of pounds and the whole team relies on their safe and timely arrival.

Due to the global logistics required the truck drivers may set off several weeks ahead of the race depending on the race calendar, teams of lorries could be setting off in opposite directions around the world. All of the containers used and carried on the trucks are a standard size that can be loaded into an aircraft cargo hold if required.

WEDNESDAY EVENTS

Media Activities

TV Crews are out filming the local town for documentary summaries that feature on Sky TV, the BBC and world press, photographers are capturing pictures of the circuit or any specially arranged PR event. In Monaco the drivers and crew may get together for a game of football or visit local venues to sign autographs.

Advertising is added to the armco around the circuit, team names go over the garages and the circuit is swept.

The Preparation Team

The pre-team are usually at the circuit approximately 4-5 days before the race starts. The team has a Race Team Manager and Support Team Manager as well as co-ordinators to take care of each area of preparation. A series of checklists need to be fully signed off to confirm the set up is correct and is paramount for the safety of the team and distinguished guests.

Setting up for race weekend is no small task and depending on the size of team, 50-100 people may support the race event. The kit man needs to ensure everyone has the sponsored and branded clothing. Then the trucks need to be emptied and a team of about 30 truckies & forklift drivers are on hand to ensure that everything is unloaded and unpacked.

Like a military mission the first thing you need to do when on the ground is establish power supplies and communication. IT systems, communications and telemetry need to be installed and full operation confirmed.

The hospitality rig needs to be built; refrigerators, catering facilities, tables & chairs need to be set up for the team and guests. Then the food and drink supplies are delivered and the chefs and caterers begin to prepare a nutritional menu.

In addition, the garage needs to be equipped, pit lane equipment installed. The fuel supplies and tyres need to be collected and taken to the garage.

Finally the teams check the weather forecasts, and confirm if any late updates are arriving for the cars so that they can begin to prepare the cars for practice.

THURSDAY EVENTS

Media

The FIA Press interview takes place for the drivers and team principles. The worlds TV & photographic press attend to get the thoughts of the drivers.

Race Preparation

The drivers will walk or cycle the track with their personal trainer and or enginers, this is not only an opportunity for exercise but to help the driver focus his mind on the race preparation and to learn the track layout at slow speed. The driver will be looking for the overtaking points, electronic signs and marshal positions that indicate the race status e.g. flag warning points, distance marker signs and bumps in the circuit that they can use to gauge track position and braking point. They also gauge the size of the kerbs to see how much of a kerb they can use. Some circuits have been updated over the years and have used different types of tarmac and the quality of the laying varies. This has a huge difference on how the tyres work on each surface and how the rain sits on the surface.

Today most race circuits have been mapped by global positioning systems (GPS) and any bump over a few centimetres can be captured, this is why driving games and F1 simulators are so representative of the circuits.

The driver reports his notes to the team principle, race engineer and lead engineers to determine the primary strategy and car set up.

The mechanics will set about updating the cars with any late updates devised by the design office that have been through the wind tunnel testing and have arrived from the manufacturing department.

Scrutineering

All cars will go through the process of scrutineering between the hours of 10:00am and 16:00pm to ensure they comply with the FIA rules and regulations. Minimum weight, safety systems and dimensional requirements will be checked as well as any innovation that may require clarification in the spirit of the rules. Each car must pass the requirements defined in the technical regulations. The scrutineering bay is the long ramp that you see the drivers walk to too get weighed after the race.

FRIDAY EVENTS

Race Weekend Programme of Events

The programme of events that take place depend on the location of the race and supporting race formulas that compete on that continent. A typical sequence of events will resemble the following schedule but supporting series may vary due to promoter commitments.

Friday	
06:00	Closure of track to traffic
08:30 to 09:15	Free practice session Formula Renault 3.5

10:00 to 11:30	1st Free Practice Session F1
12:00 to 12:30	Free practice session GP2
14:00 to 15:30	2nd Free Practice Session F1
16:15 to 16:45	GP2 – Start of the 1st Race
17:20 to 18:05	Qualifying Porsche Mobil 1 Supercup
19:00	Opening of track to traffic

Saturday	
7:00	Closure of track to traffic
09:00 to 09:25	Formula Renault 3.5 - Stage A - Qualifying sessions
09:30 to 09:55	Formula Renault 3.5 - Stage B - Qualifying sessions
11:00 to 12:00	F1 - 3rd practice session
14:00 to 15:00	F1 - Qualifying sessions
16:10 to 16:55	GP2 - Start of the 2nd Race
19:00	Opening of track to traffic

Sunday	
07:00	Closure of track to traffic
09:45 to 10:15	Porsche Supercup - Race start
11:10 to 11:55	Formula Renault 3.5 - Race Start
12:30	F1 - Drivers parade
14:00	F1 – GRAND PRIX
19:00	Opening of track to traffic

Monaco is the exception where events shown above for Friday happen on the Thursday and the Friday events would look like the following:

07:00	Closure of track to road traffic
09:30 to 10:15	Porsche Supercup - Qualifying session
11:15 to 12:15	GP2 - First Race
14:00	Opening of track to road traffic

The reason for Monaco being different is that sponsorship deals are done in Monaco and a significant amount of PR activities take place.

Many teams are sponsored by fashion companies and for the followers of the F1 circus, the girlfriends and families may spend the morning attending a PR event. The drivers will participate as models to fulfil the company's contractual agreements to show off the designer's latest clothing, jewellery, watches, shoes and after-shave. These are the images you may see published in magazines and on TV.

Friday is also when the public and press get access to the circuit and another team of people is required to begin the weekend events in earnest; the Pit Wall and Garage Team, Drivers, Support Team Manager, Drivers PA's, Drivers Managers, Head of Marketing, Head of Brand & Events, Head of Accounts, Head of Communications, Press Officer, Sponsoring Manager, Business Development Directors, Hospitality Manager, Sponsors.

The teams are on hand to ensure the sponsors get the contracted advertisement coverage they are paying for, and any outward communication to the press is controlled and information is not leaked in relation to driver or key personnel changes or technical innovation.

Members of the team must be seen wearing the sponsored hat, team watch and clothing, and any logo on display must be official, and the team employs a manager to ensure this happens.

Friday evening is likely to have a party gathering in a spectacular venue to keep the sponsors and esteemed guests entertained. In Monaco this is usually a huge yacht and many of the deals for the next years sponsorship are discussed in principle and informally at these events. The job to finalise these agreements are then handed over to the lawyers, financial director and public relations team to bring the deal to the table and ensure the company has the essential funds and sponsorship package.

Drivers

The team take 3-4 drivers to every race. No1 & No2 drivers and third seat test driver. If a driver is unable to compete, the team and the race will go on without them. No driver is bigger than the team and emotion does not form part of the decision who races and who does not. If a driver is ill or likely not to bring home the points their seat will be taken.

The third seat driver will take part in other races over the weekend like GP2 or any other event on the promoters programme. They also take part in a lot of PR activities over the race weekend with the guests and the press as well as use the opportunity of being in the garage to learn from the engineers and the mechanics how the cars have been designed and set up, and take that learning away to the next testing session. In modern F1 a driver needs to be every bit as good an engineer as the rest of the team.

Drivers 1 & 2 focus their attention on car set up and strategy until after the race when a number of PR commitments need to be met. Friday includes some free practice sessions in order to trial out the theoretical car set up in practice.

Pit Wall Team

All IT equipment, communications and data analysis on the pit wall are tested under race conditions and this is a dress rehearsal for qualifying event. There are 6-8 seats on the pit wall. The team's principle director and the chief technical director take the two central seats, the team manager will sit next to the team director and on the left and right are the drivers race engineers. The engine partner, the tyre partner, an analyst or the controls engineer for race support may occupy the remaining seats.

The Garage Crew

All the mechanics check that every tool is in its designated toolbox and in full functional order. Any tool not in your hand has to be put back in the toolbox in case any other team member needs it. This is a discipline essential when a car needs an urgent rebuild, no time must be wasted looking for tools. Tool calibrations need to be confirmed.

Tyre blankets, cooling fans, garage screen monitors, fuel pumps, laptops, data loggers and telemetry, steering wheel functions and every mechanical part of the car need to be checked. You do not leave anything to chance and ask your team-mates and crew leader to verify every action.

The driver or team principles may request modifications to the car based on updated data analysis, changing weather conditions or as a result of an accident or incident.

The driver and the pit stop team will be out in the pit lane practicing pit stops during the morning.

Back At Mission Control – Headquarters

A team of about a dozen engineers and strategists will be analyzing live data from the car based back at the team headquarters. It is not possible to take all of the equipment and databases to the circuit but these team members play a huge role. This team will be predicting tyre degradation, fuel consumption, over heating, mechanical failures, for all moving parts on the car, and running simulation models of the components and race scenario's. Other analysis teams will look at weather patterns and pit stop lap optimisation.

Based on qualifying times, qualifying position, tyres used in qualification and known parameters like vehicle weight, it is possible to calculate the fuel used in qualifying and to simulate when your competitors will pit stop.

Once a circuit and all parameters have been configured a team could run thousands of simulations making unique vehicle set up for each adjustable feature on the car. This could be as minor as minutes and degrees of angle adjustment to any wing or aerodynamic feature on the car, ride height, tyre pressure, tyre temperature, gear shift timing, track position on entrance and exit of a corner, mapping drag turbulence of your competitor and effect on the down force on your car if running in the slip stream.

Computing power and algorithm creation is now a massive part of F1; this is a great opportunity for any mathematician and software developer.

Helicopter Crew

Pilots will bring the drivers and key team members to the circuit if driving is not an option. During the race they will feeding back information on weather, forecasting and visualizing wet & dry track sectors.

Personal Trainers

It is essential that any F1 driver stays in peak physical condition. Each driver has their own dedicated personal coach, and the drivers will spend several hours every single day with their personal trainer making sure that they are building up their strength and their cardiovascular ability, and ensure they maintain the right diet. The personal trainer will look after the driver's physical conditioning, mental strength and determination to keep them focused in preparation for the race.

Caterers & Chef

When a team travels, caterers are sent with the team and are based in the hospitality truck ensuring everyone is provided the right nutritional diet to keep them at the top of their game.

When F1 travels the world it cannot afford for its pit crew team, support staff and esteemed guests and sponsors to fall ill. Everybody likes to ensure that the team is kept healthy and that everyone is fed correctly and everybody has a strict nutritional and balanced diet to keep the team at the top of their game, especially the drivers. There are careers in F1 as a chef, and a professional caterer. The McLaren Group operate a business called Absolute Taste, and this is a preferred supplier to the F1 industry.

Absolute Taste is now also recognised in several other industries now and provides catering services to celebrities and corporate organisation. Absolute Taste is based in the McLaren Technology Centre in Woking. This is obviously an ideal opportunity for somebody to choose a catering career that can take them inside an F1 company. While you are within the McLaren family as such, you have the opportunity to get a good insight into the teams, the cars, and you can look at all the history on display, the F1 cars and all the trophies on display within their technology centre. The team takes two chefs and two kitchen staff to support the race team.

So, for anybody that is a fan of F1 and enjoys catering, this is an ideal opportunity for you to combine both your professional career and your hobby.

Medical Crews

It is a requirement that medical crews attend every race event, some of these are Doctors approved by the FIA and the local motorsport organisations, but you also have a number of volunteers on hand to deal with any medical incident, not just on the track but in the crowd as well. In the UK St John's Ambulance provide support, if you are not aware St John's Ambulance is a charity and relies on donations to keep going. I am requesting that every F1 and motorsport fan put your hand in your pocket and make a donation at **http://www.sja.org.uk/sja/support-us/donate-now.aspx.** Without their support motor racing would not happen.

Air Ambulance

Air ambulance medical helicopter pilots and ambulance paramedics are also required to support the circuit. In the event of a serious incident their swift action is the difference between life and death. Please take a few minutes to look up and donate to your local air ambulance crew or visit **http://www.theairambulanceservice.org.uk/donate.**

Fire Crew

Trained firepersonnel and fire marshals may also be some of the first people to the scene of an accident. We all recognise the danger of fire and the injuries that can be suffered. Niki Lauda's injuries were a terrible reminder of the dangers of motorsport. Please support the open days and community events to donate to your local fire crew or visit **http://www.firefighterscharity.org.uk.**

SATURDAY QUALIFYING

Preparation for qualifying is similar to Friday practice for the garage team. However for the team principle and the analysts and mission control this is a big day, this is the first indication of the competitor's true pace. You not only monitor your own cars performance but capture data on sector and lap times, tyre choices and take weather readings. In addition walk the pit lane to look over the set up of competitors cars and see if there is anything illegal fitted to the car that could result in disqualification or grid place penalty. This might sound like a devious tactic but the rules were created for fairness.

You have to get your strategy right for qualifying so that you do not compromise your race strategy for Sunday. A good comprehension of the rules is essential and strangely due to the tyre rule of needing to use each compound you might benefit by not qualifying in the top 10 positions so that you can change your car set up for a better race strategy.

The driver and the race engineer will be looking over all performance data for themselves and the other team driver to see who is quickest. Each corner and speed down the straights is studied, when KER's and DRS were used, top speed achieved, when they lifted the throttle and rpm dropped, when the gear shift took place and how long the shift took. Shifting time is not so much of an issue in a modern gearbox where the gear change is predicted and primed for a shift. The driver also looks to adjust when they turned into the corner to see if they can reduce lateral loads on the tires to prolong their life, and when they got back on the throttle as this leaves a trace in the telemetry data.

You look at the infrared images of the tyres to see if you are overheating them in relation to your team mate. Keeping the tyres in the optimum operational window is now one of the biggest factors to lap time, cold tyres do not grip the track like a warm tire, hot tyres get soft and scrub rubber reducing the duration of use. The data can be overlaid on your teammates data to see the optimum timing and sequence of actions for the driver to follow.

The qualifying format does change from time to time, but currently it is run in three sessions.

1. Q1 requires all 22 drivers to put in a qualifying lap in a 20 minute session and the slowest 6 drivers are eliminated from the remaining qualifying sessions. These will form the back end of the grid. F1 has a minimum time requirement for qualifying, any driver exceeding 107 percent of the fastest cars time cannot compete in the race. This is to prevent a large disparity in speed on the circuit and is a safety requirement. Driver's eliminated in Q1 are able to modify their car set up for the race. Cars will be chosen at random for scrutineering checks.

2. Q2 takes place after a 7 minute recess and the remaining 16 cars compete in a 15 minute session in an attempt to qualify for Q3. The slowest 6 drivers take the places 11-16 on the grid. Driver's eliminated in Q2 are able to modify their car set up for the race. Cars will be chosen at random for scrutineering checks.

3. Q3 is the battle for pole position and to start from the front of the grid. It is a 15 minutes session to set the fastest time but drivers cannot modify their car after this qualifying session. You start the race as per your qualifying car set up. The cars are placed in Parc Ferme, translated to English this is park closes. It means that the cars are parked and covered up so that you cannot get access to them. All cars that competed in Q3 will be measured, weighed and checked by the FIA scrutineering crew.

After qualifying the drivers must attend the FIA Press Conference to talk about how the qualification sessions worked out for them.

SUNDAY RACE DAY

Other promotional events occur like a London Route Master bus sponsored by the UK government may lap the circuit to promote UK business overseas. You may ask why the government is in on the act? The UK government ensures supplies of materials, minerals and energy used by UK industry keep coming. F1 demands the supply of leading technologies and innovative suppliers to lead the global technical innovation.

In the hours leading up to the race the track is occupied with other races like GP2 and the future stars of F1 prove out their talent and start to increase their fan base. The driver's parade is a time honoured tradition before the grand prix and a time for the crowd to photograph their idols.

When the PR events have finished the cars are pushed out of the garage on to the grid. Pit girls mark the location for each car based on the qualifying position and any adjustments made to grid positions by the FIA for infringements of the rules.

Pit Girls

The Pit Girls are all models hired by the promoter of the circuit. They may participate in some of the fashion PR events but are primarily hired to stand at the front of the cars on the grid and hold the team and car number signs. After the race they form a guard of honour for the drivers as they walk to the podium. It probably also comes as no surprise that the pit girls may become the future wives and girlfriends for people working in F1.

The Grid

As long as everyone qualified within 107% of the fastest car, 22 cars will line up on the grid. We have all seen the TV presenters and press running up and down the grid to get interviews and pictures with the drivers, engineers and any celebrities, you only get access to the grid if you have pit pass access or are a member of the Paddock Club.

Some drivers are happy to talk to the press but for others this is the last opportunity for a comfort break, it has been known for drivers needing an opportunity to lose fluids during the race to use the car for convenience.

For others this is the time when they blank out the distractions and start to go through the mental preparation process. The driver's mental preparation can begin as they start to dress in the race wear.

Each layer of clothing starting with the fire resistant Nomex FIA 8856-2000 approved Underwear is like putting on an invincibility suit of armour. If you approach the race thinking you were going to get hurt you may hold back and not rely on science behind the cars design and performance and the quality of the safety equipment. This could lead to you making a mistake and the creation of a self-fulfilled prophecy.

The race suit and boots may be about a feeling of self well-being. I am at the top of my game; I look the part, I feel good, and this is a moment of relaxation and taking in the atmosphere, walking to the grid and assuring yourself with the help of your lead mechanic that the car is complete and ready to deliver the premium ride.

As the helmet goes on and HANs device attached all distractions are removed, and the driver enters the car. The belts are applied and the driver and the car become one. The driver checks the settings of the car on the steering well and the bond of trust is formed.

The final stage of preparation is thinking about the start, the lap and track positions, making a mental prediction of where your competitors will move. If Sebastian Vettel is on the outside of the track in Pole position he will move to the middle of the track to form a blockage before moving back to the outside for the corner line. As the driver puts on the gloves this is preparation complete, this is what I do, it's time to go to work.

The teams aim to keep the car primed to a race condition as much as possible. The tyres are wrapped with heating blankets. Once the engine has been cranked and is running, cooling fans are used to manage the temperature of the car while it is stationary.

Five red lights on the start indicate the warm up lap is about to get underway. This is when you see the frenzy of activity as the teams and their equipment move to the edge of the track and cars pull away for warm up lap.

THE RACE EVENT

Each car is fitted with a sensor to detect a jump-start. Every driver should know exactly where the sensor is on their car so that they do not compromise the start of their race. If this sensor was located near the front of the car a small lunge forward when selecting gear could be called a jump-start. The driver may also be able to try and push the envelope and predict when the fifth red light will go out and gain a fraction of a second on the competitors.

Once started the whole race is a continuous loop of monitoring and analysis by the team to keep the race strategy operating to its maximum potential.

The race has a maximum duration of two hours or that the car must cover a minimum number of laps exceeding 305 km. The Monaco Grand Prix is the only exception to this rule where 260 km must be covered. This is because Monaco is a street circuit and you can not achieve the race distance in the 2 hour maximum window.

RACE STRATEGY

Over the course of a season on average the cars will burn 3.3litres of fuel per lap and this equates to 2.4kg of weight reduced per lap, and each kg of fuel adds 0.03 seconds to a lap. The car must finish the race with a weight not less than 642kg including the weight of the driver. The driver would weigh approximately 75kg.

The Monaco Grand Prix is 78 laps x 3.340 km per lap = 260km

In 2013 the fastest lap time was 1'16.577 or 76.577 seconds on lap 77.

The Fuel Laps Weight Effect is:

2.4kg x 0.03s = 0.072 seconds per lap.

3.3 litres = 2.4kg = 0.072 seconds per lap.

Fuel used in a Race is 78 laps x 3.3 litres = 257.4 litres

Starting Weight is 78 laps x 2.4kg = 187.2kg + 642kg = 829kg (including driver)

Fuel Time Effect is 78 laps x 0.072 seconds = 5.616 seconds

In 2014 the 1.6 litre V6 turbo engines will produce 600bhp at the output shaft. Assuming the power to weight ratio and an approximate formula of HP = Torque x RPM / 5252 this will give the car an approximate 0-60 time to the first corner of 1.927 seconds. This is an approximate sum because traffic, gear ratio, tyre temperatures and traction are not factored.

An approximate time on lap 1 would be 76.577s + 5.616s + 1.927s = 84.12 seconds lap or 1'24.12 seconds.

Lap 2 – 76.577s + 5.586s = 82.163 seconds or 1'22.163s and the time would reduce by 0.03s per lap for fuel and 2.4kg of weight per lap.

You would continue to lose weight and increase speed until you can achieve a lap of 1'16.577 or 76.577 seconds on lap 78. That's the basic principle.

You also need to add the time for the pit stops, and calculate the time from entering the pit lane and speed restriction zone, time taken changing tyres and carrying out repairs or adjustments and exit time. This may be 20-30 seconds depending on circuit.

The above is very approximate and the teams use complex mathematical algorithms and databases in which to set up race strategy scenarios and monitor and alter based on every sector time and event.

HOW A FORMULA 1 PIT STOP WORKS

The Decision To Stop

The team will inform the driver that they need to stop, this decision will be based on a number of factors and the driver is informed by holding a pit board over the pit wall and by communicating over the team radio. The driver may also tell the team that he needs to stop based on how the car is performing.

It is currently a mandatory requirement that teams use all of the tyre types selected for the race weekend, and the team would usually have worked out a strategy of how far a particular tyre will last into the race. This strategy is changed over the course of the race and getting the pit stop right is critical to success. It takes a big team of skilled engineers and analysts to decide when the optimum pit stop should take place and the contributing factors for the decision are as follows:

- **Tyre Wear** – Heavy tyre wear can be caused by high temperatures or scrubbing off rubber cornering, braking too hard and putting a flat spot on the tyre which affects the handling of the car, in any case if the handling is off or tyre has worn past its prime, lap times increase and its time to pit.
- **Puncture** – A simple hole in the tyre, pit immediately before flailing rubber damages your car.
- **Telemetry & Data Analysis** – Each car is constantly monitored for performance and sector times, but also for indicators of

potential system failures. A series of sensor and software are used to check the health of the car to highlight remedial action that may be required.

- **Race Simulation** – Each team monitors the other teams lap times and simulates when they will pit. They also predict who will be on the track at the end of the pit lane when their driver re-joins the race. Putting your car out on an empty track gives you time to get the tyres up to race temperature without losing time and position.
- **Track Position** – Each team would like to keep its driver in clean air and avoid being stuck in the dirty air of another car as this leads to slower lap times and increased tyre wear. If you cannot pass a car and a tyre change is due, get in and get out in clean air.
- **Weather** – Rain means that it is time to get off the slick tyres and get on the intermediate wet or full wet tyres. Being out on the wrong tyres will kill your race.
- **Broken Bodywork** – You can live with some damage but broken nose or rear wing require immediate action or you may lose aerodynamic down force.
- **Safety Car** – A major incident has occurred, race pace is slowed down and the drivers will be forced to bunch up and follow the safety car, this is the time to pit so that you do not lose race pace or distance when the race is at full speed.
- **Drive Through Penalty or Stop and Go Penalty** – The team cannot carry out any work to the car but they do have a window of laps in which to choose when to bring the car in. While this is a penalty, with good data you look to minimise the effect. For the stop and go penalty this is in the hands of the Go No Go lollipop man. Michael Schumacher once finished his race in the pit lane by serving his stop and go on the final lap winning the race. This took a good knowledge of the rules from a strategist to make this call.

The Pit Box

The pit box is two straight lines indicating the length of the car, with two lines painted at 90 degrees on each line indicating the approximate length of the cars wheel base in the x axis (front to back) and the tyre position, and the width of the car (y axis), at the entrance of the box two line at 45 degrees are painted and the pit crew should try not exceed the limit of these lines with the exception of the jack men and the nose and rear wing men. The lines are there to indicate a safety point to avoid the pit crew being run over by their own driver or that of another team. It also ensures that a working space in the pit lane is equally divided for each team.

The Pit Stop

Front Jack Man is positioned centrally in front of the arriving car, the driver aligns the centre of the car to his position as he arrives into the pit box, the driver cannot see the end of the nose so the front tyre removal men hold up stop signs that is mounted to his forearm so that the driver knows where to stop the car in the box in relation to the 90 degree line.

Once the car has stopped and sometimes just a fraction of a second before, the nut men on all 4 corners are undoing the nuts. The driver keeps his foot on the brake during the pit stop. The front jack man uses a cantilever jack to raise the nose, in parallel to this the rear jack man who is stood by the 45 degree line on the outside of the pit lane steps in and places his jack ready to hoist the car.

4x men are used to stabilise the car whilst it is in the air, it has only been jacked on the centre line so could roll in the y axis (left to right). Two are positioned at the front wing and two positioned holding the side pods and engine cover. The front wing men will also make adjustments to the down force settings of the wing, and the side pod men will clear debris from the side pods.

The nut men remove the nut guns and nut, and the jack men hoist the car. The tyre removal men then step in. On the front of the car the removal men are stood between the nut men and the wingmen and remove the tyre to the front of the car rolling it with them as they step backwards still facing the car, this is because there is not enough room to turn and walk away.

On the rear of the car the tyre removal men are stood between the tyre and side pod, they have the choice of rolling the tyre and stepping backwards or turning their back to car.

The tyre fitters initial step close to the tyre being removed holding the new tyre at the same height and an angle of about 45 degrees, ready to rotate the tyre onto the hub. The hub usually has a lead in chamfer and a coloured band to help the fitter visually align the tyre, and the hub then guides the wheel alignment.

The nut men change the rotational direction of the nut gun when the tyre is being removed and are ready to place the nut back onto the thread as the tyre fitter is guiding the wheel into place. The nut man begins to fit the nut with the car still in the air and at this point the driver is selecting gear. The jack men drop the car and the pit crew move back behind the safety lines. The Go No Go lollipop man is monitoring the pit lane for traffic and indicates to the driver to light the fires and spin the tyres and exit the box.

That's how you pit stop in circa 4 seconds.

Pit Stop Crew

1x Front Jack Man
1x Rear Jack Man
1x Go No Go Lollipop Man may be used by some teams, others use a light system.
4x teams of tyre men – 1 x nut man, 1 x tyre removal man, 1 x tyre fitter = 12 people
2x Nose & Front Wing men to adjust settings
2 x Side Pod Men to stabilise car and clear debris from side pods.

2x Rear Wing Men on stand by in case of damage.
Depending on regulations sometimes 2 x fuel men.
Other mechanics will look over the car for any other signs of damage.

THE PRESENTATION

Before walking out to the podium the drivers are required to wear clothing provided by the sponsors of the race. The drivers must ensure their race overalls are displaying the team and driver sponsorship brands and they also have to put on a hat and a watch before leaving the preparation room.

The national anthem for the winning driver is played first, followed by the team national anthem. Esteemed guests and dignitaries award the trophies to the three podium drivers and the winning constructor.

The champagne bottle is a jeroboam meaning a 3 litre bottle, interestingly the tradition of spraying champagne didn't begin in F1, the F1 drivers used to take civilised sip from the bottle. Spraying the champagne actually began at the 24 hour Le Mans race in 1967 when Dan Gurney from the Shelby-American Team in a moment of joy and excitement started spraying his team members. Since then it has been adopted as a tradition in all Formula.

After Race Interviews

After the trophies have been awarded the drivers must also attend an interview for the worlds press. This used to be conducted in a conference room but is now conducted on the podium in front of the public crowd, the press and the team members. The journalists and TV presenters ask questions about the race to gain the drivers perspective. This session provides the stories for the press articles and is a great opportunity to promote the event.

The After Party

After the race is complete its time to pack away the tools and equipment and lock the garages. It is also time to party, and no one parties like F1. Stages have been built and some of the biggest bands in the world hired. For the esteemed guests and for the F1 crews it is time to relax and have a good time. There are a number of musically talented team members in F1 that are prepared to get on stage and play a set. Despite the competitiveness a sense of family exists throughout the pit lane.

Once the weekend events are over, once the trucks are packed and the team has departed it is time to start the cycle over again. The cars are returned to factory and every part is dismantled and inspected for damage or failure, testing is carried out in some cases to learn how the improve the design for the next race.

23. A FEW FINAL WORDS

This book was written to give you an insight to jobs that exist in F1, to inspire you to follow your dream of working in F1, and to match a career to your ambition and abilities whether you have a degree or not. A career is something you work for, it is not built in a day and it will not be handed to you on a plate. Your career is your choice to make, and it relies on you making informed and educated decisions, I hope that the information contained in this book has helped you to see your opportunity to get involved. Get motivated to take action and make it a reality.

You have now reached the end of the book and no doubt will be ready to start planning and preparing your career for a job in F1. Write your plan down, put it on the wall, look at it every day and check your progress. Make good use of the tools provided to support you at **www.jobsinf1.com** and reward yourself for your progress.

I would like to wish you all the best of luck and I sincerely hope that you have the strength of character and commitment to fulfil your dream. Please remember you make your own luck and it is born from preparation.

We are all individual, so why be ordinary.

Stephen Sawyer

24. ABBREVIATIONS & ACCRONYMS

1. ADR (Accident Data Recorder)
2. APQP (Advanced Project Quality Planning)
3. ARDS Association of Racing Drivers
4. ARKS Association of Racing Karts
5. BOM (Bill of Materials)
6. BRDC British Racing Drivers Club
7. BRSCC British Racing Sports Car Club
8. CAD (Computer Aided Design)
9. CAE (Computer Aided Engineering)
10. CAM (Computer Aided Modelling)
11. CFD (Computational Fluid Dynamics)
12. CNC Machinist (Computer Numerically Controlled)
13. DFMEA (Design Failure Mode Element Analysis)
14. DVP (Design Validation Plan)
15. DRS (Drag Reduction System)
16. ECU (Electronic Control Unit)
17. EDS (Electrical Distribution System)
18. EMC (Electro Magnetic Compatibility)
19. EMS (Engine Management System)
20. ERS (Energy Recovery System)
21. FEA (Finite Element Analysis)
22. FIA (Fédération Internationale de l'Automobile)

23. FIA World Motor Sport Council WMSC
24. FOCA Formula One Constructors Association
25. FOM Formula One Management (Film Crew)
26. FOTA (Formula One Team Association)
27. G's (Gravity – This is a force that can be applied in any direction)
28. GPS (Global Positioning System)
29. HANS (Head & Neck Support)
30. HIC (Head Impact Calculation)
31. HIL (Hardware In Loop)
32. KERS (Kinetic Energy Recover System)
33. MMI (Man Machine Interface)
34. MSA (Motor Sport Association)
35. OEM (Original Equipment Manufacture)
36. PFMEA (Process Failure Mode Element Analysis)
37. PPAP (Production Part Approval Process)
38. PSW (Part Submission Warrant)
39. RSF (Racing Steps Foundation)
40. SIL (Systems In Loop)
41. VA VE (Value Added Value Engineering)

25. IMAGES

If you would like to purchase any of the images in this book please use the following links and contact Russell Batchelor at **XPB.CC**

Jenson Button (GBR) McLaren in parc ferme. 12.10.2013. Formula 1 World Championship, Rd 15, Japanese Grand Prix, Suzuka, Japan, Qualifying Day.

Jenson Button (GBR) McLaren at the Amber Lounge Fashion Show. 24.05.2013. Formula 1 World Championship, Rd 6, Monaco Grand Prix, Monte Carlo, Monaco, Friday.

The helmet of Jenson Button (GBR) McLaren. 31.01.2013. McLaren MP4-28 Launch, McLaren Technology Centre, Woking, England.

The New Lotus E21 28.01.2013. Lotus F1. Lotus E21 Launch, Enstone, England.

Nico Rosberg (GER), Mercedes GP 12.10.2013. Formula 1 World Championship, Rd 15, Japanese Grand Prix, Suzuka, Japan, Qualifying Day.

Will Buxton (GBR) NBS Sports Network TV Presenter with Sebastian Vettel (GER) Red Bull Racing. 18.04.2013. Formula 1 World Championship, Rd 4, Bahrain Grand Prix, Sakhir, Bahrain, Preparation Day.

McLaren celebrate 50 years as a constructor on their motor-home. 05.09.2013. Formula 1 World Championship, Rd 12, Italian Grand Prix, Monza, Italy, Preparation Day.

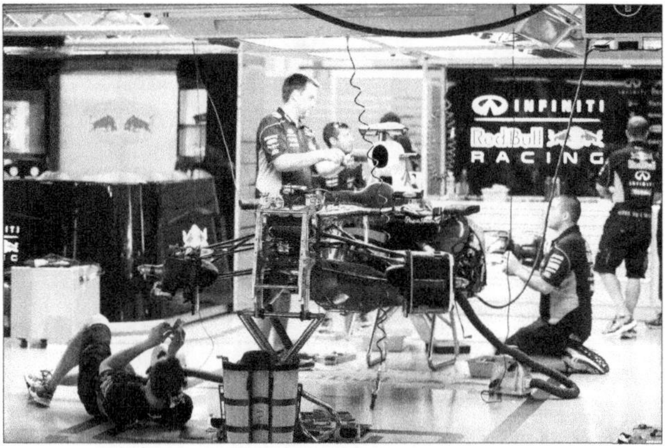

Red Bull Racing RB9 is prepared in the pits. 19.09.2013. Formula 1 World Championship, Rd 13, Singapore Grand Prix, Singapore, Singapore, Preparation Day.

Jenson Button (GBR), McLaren Mercedes 30.06.2013. Formula 1 World Championship, Rd 8, British Grand Prix, Silverstone, England, Race Day.

The start of the race. 22.09.2013. Formula 1 World Championship, Rd 13, Singapore Grand Prix, Singapore, Singapore, Race Day.

Mark Webber (AUS) Red Bull Racing RB9 makes a pit stop. 27.10.2013. Formula 1 World Championship, Rd 16, Indian Grand Prix, New Delhi, India, Race Day.

Race winner and World Champion Sebastian Vettel (GER) Red Bull Racing celebrates on the podium. 27.10.2013. Formula 1 World Championship, Rd 16, Indian Grand Prix, New Delhi, India, Race Day.

Race winner Fernando Alonso (ESP) Ferrari celebrates on the podium. 14.04.2013. Formula 1 World Championship, Rd 3, Chinese Grand Prix, Shanghai, China, Race Day.

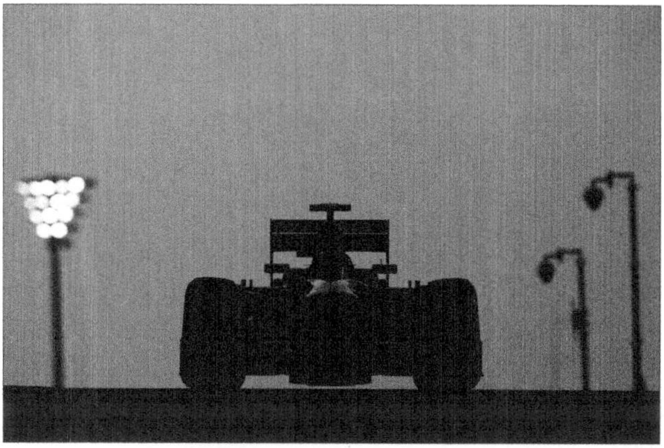

Lewis Hamilton (GBR) Mercedes AMG F1 W04. 02.11.2013.
Formula 1 World Championship, Rd 17, Abu Dhabi Grand Prix,
Yas Marina Circuit, Abu Dhabi, Qualifying Day.

26. INDEX